CONTRIBUTIONS TO SANSKRIT CRITICISM

CONTRIBUTIONS TO SANSKRIT CRITICISM

(Collection of Papers of Professor A.C. Swain)

Editor

DR. SIDDHESWAR JENA

Principal

N.C. Autonomous College, Jajpur.

BKP

BHARATIYA KALA PRAKASHAN

DELHI (INDIA)

First Published : 2007

ISBN : 978-81-8090-128-7

Published by : **C.P. Gautam**
for **BHARATIYA KALA PRAKASHAN**
3421-A, IInd Floor, Narang Colony,
Tri Nagar, Delhi-110035.
Phone : 27393083, 32967505
Email : bkp3421@yahoo.co.in

Laser Typesetting by : Twinkle Graphics, Delhi-110088.

Printed by BDH Printers at D. K. Fine Art Press, Delhi

Contents

Contents

Preface

Prof. Dr. Anam Charan Swain was Professor and Head of the Department of Sanskrit in the Post-Graduate Department of Sanskrit, Utkal University, Bhubaneswar for long twelve years. A devoted teacher, an able administrator and above all a keen researcher he has produced some fifteen Ph.D. students including the present editor to his credit. As a distinguished scholar of Sanskrit of Orissa after his superannuation he has received the President's Award of Certificate of Honour.

In the year 1925 Dr. Swain had his birth in a land-owner's family with a silver spoon in his mouth. His grand father was a devout follower of *Mahimā-dharma*. The followers of this faith are well-known as *śunyavādins* and they believe in the absolute supremacy of *śunya-brahman*. In conformity with the trend of the faith, *anāma* (nameless), *alekha* (unwritten) and *aṇākāra* (formless) are the most popular terms (designations of the absolute) prevalent in this cult. And the young child was christened "Anāma" by Śrī Viśvanātha Bābā, the then oldest and wisest sannyāsin of Mahimā-dharma following the age-long tradition of the family.

Born in a small village called "Byree" Dr. Swain had his primary education in the local school. He matriculated from Pyarimohan Academy and graduated from Ravenshaw College, Cuttack with First Class Hons. in Sanskrit. Then he went to B.H.U. for his Post-Graduate Studies. In the M.A. Examination he topped the list in his batch and joined the Orissa Education Service as Lecturer in the year 1949.

After a few years of Government Service he went abroad and came to be the first research student of Prof. H.H. Ingalls at Harvard University, U.S.A. He completed his Ph.D. degree there and came back to India in the year 1957. For a simple and unsophisticated young man like him born and brought up in the village surroundings it was really a long march from Byree to far-off Boston.

He qualified for University job and joined Utkal University as Reader-in-Sanskrit in 1958. In 1973 he was promoted to the post of Professor and continued as the Head of the Department of Sanskrit since then till his retirement in 1985.

Prof. Swain is a thorough scholar in Sanskrit language and literature. Whatever text he teaches or goes through, he goes very deeply into the problem. His analysis of things is very clear and distinct. Though he obtained his Ph.D. degree on a philosophical topic entitled "Saṅkara's Concept of Creation" (Unpublished), after coming back from the United States he switched over to the Purāṇa Literature and proved himself to be a scholar of repute in this branch.

As his name suggests, Prof. Swain never boasts of his erudition. Whatever he knows, he knows it perfectly and accurately. It is his nature not to float on the surface, but to go to the root of a problem. He meekly admits his ignorance before others in case he does not know some point. He firmly believes in the oft-quoted adage–"न हि सर्वः सर्वं वेत्ति" (All of us do not know all things).

This work is a collection of handful of research papers written by Prof. Swain. The papers were published in different journals of India long back. Though the work is a small one, still it is a valuable contribution to the field of Sanskrit criticism. When one goes through this work, one must, I am sure, be impressed by the thorough analysis and the critical remarks of the author. The papers still retain their importance and offer an easy pleasurable reading.

Now Prof. Swain is an octogenarian. May he live long! We pray Lord Jagannātha, the national deity of our state to grant him many more years to be with us, his students.

Lastly Mr. C.P. Gautam, Bharatiya Kala Prakashan, Delhi deserves all praise for his prompt and neat publication of this work.

15 August 2006 **SIDDHESWAR JENA**
Bubaneshwar

Chapter 1

Concept of Hiraṇyagarbha in the Philosophy of Saṃkara

The monistic teaching of *Śaṃkara*, although centering on one absolute entity, accepts the existence of various *Īśvaras*, personifications of natural forces and natural phenomenon, as described in the Ṛg Veda. These gods or *Īśvaras*, like Fire, Sun, etc., are the protectors of the world. High above all these gods stands *Īśvara* or more specifically *Parameśvara* as the eternal god. In between *Parameśvara* and the lesser-*Īśvaras* like Fire, Sun etc., there are also other gods like *Hiraṇyagarbha* and *Virāj*. According to Paul Deussen* the belief in various gods evidenced by the *Mīmāṁsa Karmakāṇḍa* was responsible for the introduction of these gods into the monistic system of *Śaṃkara*.

Brahman, the supreme entity is impersonal, a homogeneous mass of objectless thought, transcending all attributes, whereas *Īśvara* is *Brahman* associated with the unreal principle of *māyā*. This *Īśvara* is the world-projecting God standing first in the hierarchic emanation of different forms of life appearing at the beginning of each aeon.

The next emanation in the order of descent is *Hiraṇyagarbha*. He is at the head of all gods like fire, Sun, etc., the personified personal deities, who, being fearful of *Īśvara*, have been busy in their daily run of activities. Like these gods, *Hiraṇyagarbha owed his existence and glory to* Īśvara. He perishes (ceases to function) at the end of each world cycle (*kalpa*), and is reborn (begins to function) at the beginning of the new world cycle (*kalpa*). *Hiraṇyagarbha* is one of those gods who continue the same sort of existence which they enjoyed in the previous world cycle, because they are distinguished by superior knowledge and power of action (*B.S.Bh.*1.3.30. p. 293.3-6). *Hiraṇyagarbha* is the first creation of *Parameśvara*. He is the first born (*prathamaja*, *B.S.Bh.*1.4.1. p. 33.3-5). He is also the first embodied one (*śarīrī prathamah*). The threefold world is the body of *Hiraṇyagarbha*. He is called *Puruśa* (*B.S.Bh.*1.2.23. p. 206.16; p. 207.3). *Hiraṇyagarbha* is at the highest point where the manifestation of knowledge and lordship is at the fullest (*B.S.Bh.*1.3.30. p. 293.1-2). His superiority of knowledge is attested by the fact that *Īśvara* delivered all the Vedas to him at the beginning of creation (*B.S.Bh.*1.3.30. p. 293.6-7). He is the support of all the worlds comprising the *adhyātma,* the *adhibhūta* and the *adhidaiva* (*Katha.Up.Bh.*2.11. p. 41.10-11; p. 42.4). But this state of *Hiraṇyagarbha*, though fearless, boundless and the combination of many desirable powers, yet falls within the sphere of *saṁsāra*. This is why *Naciketas* rejects it (*Katha.Up.Bh.*2.11. p. 42.4-8). All the kinds of bliss beginning with that of a king on earth to that of Gods like Indra and Bṛhaspati become one in *Hiraṇyagarbha* (*yatra ete ānandabhedā ekatām gachhanti*). *Hiraṇyagarbha* is not only the centre of infinite varieties of bliss; he is also the centre of virtue, knowledge and unsurpassed freedom from desire (*Tait.Up. Bh.*2.8. p. 74.18-20). The intellect of *Hiraṇyagarbha* is the basis of all intellects (*B.S.Bh.*1.4.1. p. 330.5).

In the creation of this phenomenal universe by the world-projecting deity *Īśvara*, the first entity to appear is *Hiraṇyagarbha*, though he is the second in the hierarchical emanation of *Brahman*. Like a tree growing from seed, this tree of *saṁsāra* grows from the seed of ignorance, desire, *karma* and *avyakta*. And *Hiraṇyagarbha* is the sprout of this tree of *saṁsāra* (*hiraṇyagarbhāṅkura*, *Katha.Up.Bh.*6.1. p. 104.4.5). *Hiraṇyagarbha* is born from *Brahman,* characterised by knowledge, etc. He was born before any of the five elements was produced (*Katha.Up. Bh.*4.6. p. 82.9-12). He is, as it were, the sprouting seed of the totality of cosmic ignorance, desire, *karma* and beings (*avidyā-kāma-karma-bhūta-samudāya-bījāṅkura*, *Mu.Up.Bh.*1.1.8.

p. 104.4-5). "The manifestation of the unmanifested world is the birth of *Hiraṇyagarbha*, the *sūtrātman", B.A.Up.Bh.*5.5.1 (p. 717.15; p. 718.7). Thus, within the realm of *saṁsāra* Hiraṇyagarbha is the first entity to be produced.

Hiraṇyagarbha, though himself a created entity, helps *Īśvara* in the creation of the universe. He is the creator of all (*sarvasya srastṛ, B. A.Up.Bh.*5.5.1. p. 718.7). Hiraṇyagarbha creates the bodies of gods, and enters the *ākāśa* of the heart of every living being, perceiving sound, etc. (*Katha.Up.Bh.*4.6. p. 82.12-13). All the protectors of the world are born from him (*Ait.Up.Bh.*5.3. p. 82.4). He is the primal creator of beings. He established the earth and the sky (*B.S.Bh.*1.2.23. p. 207.1.4).

Hiraṇyagarbha is the cosmic self which comes between *Īśvara* and the individual self. This Hiraṇyagarbha is looked upon as related to the universe in the same way as the individual self is related to the body. The subtle bodies of the individual transmigratory selves are strung together in the subtle self of Hiraṇyagarbha. Therefore, he is called *jīvaghana* (dense with lives, *P. Up.Bh.*5.5. p. 49.8-10). Until the effected universe is evolved, the cosmic intelligence, Hiraṇyagarbha, has for its vehicle the totality of subtle bodies. He is the living principle of all bodies. Like the image of the sun reflected in various waters, Hiraṇyagarbha enters into the limiting adjuncts of inner organs when the physical universe is evolved (*Ait. Up.Bh.* p. 81.5-6; p. 82.3). He is the Self of all organs (*karaṇātman*), and of individual selves, and dwells in the *brahma-loka*. Therefore, this *brahmaloka* also is called *jīvaghana*, as all individual selves are comprised within this Hiraṇyagarbha (*B.S.Bh.*1.3.13. p. 244.3-4).

Hiraṇyagarbha should be meditated upon with one's whole heart. Gods who are produced from Virāj, meditate upon him even to the supersession of their immediate creator Virāj (*B.A.Up.Bh.*5.5.1. p. 718.11-12). But for men, individual meditation on Hiraṇyagarbha or *Avyākṛta* (same as *Prakṛti* or *avidyā*) is disparaged. Those who meditate on *Avyākṛta* alone, fall into darkness. And those who meditate only on Hiraṇyagarbha fall into greater darkness. It is better to combine the meditation of *Avyākṛta Prakṛti* and Hiraṇyagarbha. By meditation on Hiraṇyagarbha one overcomes the defects of vice, desires and limited powers, and attains *aṇimā* and other superhuman powers. After overcoming one's limitations, one should then meditate on Prakṛti, whereby one becomes absorbed into Prakṛti. This absorption into Prakṛti is called by Śaṁkara immortality (*amṛtatva*) in a sense different from its natural meaning. This immortality of absorption into Prakṛti is relative; it can be achieved by the wealth of men and deities; and it falls within the realm of *saṁsāra* (*Īśa. U.P. Bh.* 12-14, p. 15. 11-23; p. 16.5-13). Ignorant men attached to sons and relatives, as a result of their *karma*, sacrifices, etc. go to heaven, but again enter into this world according to the residue of their *karma*. But of those hermits of the forest and **sannyāsins** who practise the **karma** enjoined in their particular order of life, and meditate on Hiraṇyagarbha, the good and bad deeds are consumed. They go to *satya-loka,* the world of Hiraṇyagarbha (*Mu.Up.Bh.*1.2.11. p. 16-17-24; p. 17.4). This *satya-loka* is the same as *brahmaloka* often referred to by *Saṁkara. Brahma-loka* is the goal of those who know the lower Brahman like Hiraṇyagarbha or the qualified *Īśvara*. He who meditates on the *Puruṣa* in the Sun (Hiraṇyagarbha) through the symbol of 'Om', becomes united with the bright Sun. Even if he meditates upon this at the last moment of his life, he does not return from the solar world as well as from the lunar world, but for ever is united with the Sun. As a snake sloughs its skin and becomes new, so is a man who meditates on the Sun; he is conducted up to the world of Hiraṇyagarbha (*P.Up.Bh.*5.5 p. 47.13, p. 48.6-10; p. 49.4-8.)

Śaṃkara makes a differentiation between householders who have only performed sacrifices, but have not meditated on the five fires or on Hiraṇyagarbha, and householders who have a knowledge of the five fires and who have meditated on Hiranyagarbha or *satya-brahma*. After death the individual selves of the former class follow the path of the manes (*pitṛ-yāna*) and go to the world of the manes (*pitṛ-loka*). From there they again return through the conditioned states of the rain-god, etc. and are again born in this world. Thus they are destined to the fate of coming and going between this world and the next. But householders of the latter class, who have meditated on Hiraṇyagarbha during their lifetime although without any effective realisation of the Supreme Self, follow the path of the gods (*deva-yāna*) after giving up their mortal bodies. In this posthumous journey they pass through different states. First they reach the deity of flame stationed in the northern part. From this deity they reach the diety of the day; then the diety of the bright fortnight, in which the moon waxes; from there they reach the group of six deities identified with the six months in which the Sun travels northward; from them the deity identified with the world of the gods; from him the Sun; thence the diety of lightning. When these householders reach the deity of lightning, an inhabitant of *brahma-loka*, a being created from the mind of Brahman (not the Supreme Brahman, but the conditioned Brahman, Hiraṇyagarbha, which Śaṃkara designates as *satya-brahma*) comes and conducts them to *brahma-loka*, the world of Hiraṇyagarbha. There are higher and lower planes in this world of Hiraṇyagarbha. And one goes to the higher or lower plane depending upon the quality of one's meditation on Hiraṇyagarbha. Being conducted to *brahma-loka* they attain perfection there and live in those worlds for many divine years, that is, many human cycles, which constitute the life time of Brahmā (*B.A. Up. Bh.*6.2.15). So in speaking of *brahma-loka* as the final goal of those who meditate on Hiraṇyagarbha, Śaṃkara does not mean Brahman the Supreme Self, but only its derivative Brahmā, who is the qualified Brahman (*saguna-brahma*), and as such considered to be the effect to the productive will of the Supreme principle (*kārya-brahma*). In this case Brahmā is identical with Hiraṇyagarbha. The state of the assimilation of the individual self to Hiraṇyagarbha in which it may remain until the end of the cycle, is what is most usually meant by *brahma-loka.* The attainment of *brahma-loka* is simply an indefinite prolongation of individual life, transposed into the subtle order and extending to the *pralaya.* To go further and to free oneself entirely from the conditions of life and duration which are inherent in individuality, there is no other path but that of knowledge of the higher kind conferring immediate deliverance. In this case there is no longer occasion to consider a passage at death to various higher, though still transitory and conditioned states.

Those who have a certain inferior knowledge or the knowledge of the conditioned Brahman like Hiraṇyagabha or *Īśvara*, attain the state of Hiraṇyagarbha or reach *Īśvara*. Those who know the highest Brahman become on their death one with it, without having resort to any other place. This distinction between reaching Hiraṇyagarbha or Īśvara on the one hand and being one with the highest Brahman on the other results from Śaṃkara's distinction between *parā vidyā* and *aparā vidyā*. According to Śaṃkara, he who knows the highest Brahman becomes at death one with it. So whenever a scriptural passage speaks of the individual self as travelling the path of the gods or as passing out of the body through some opening, etc., Śaṃkara interprets this as expressing the result of inferior knowledge. Where an individual self has attained inferior knowledge, Hiranyagarbha or Īśvara, not the highest Brahman becomes its goal, after death. The attainment of Hiraṇyagarbha or Īśvara is the result of *aparā vidyā*.

Hiraṇyagarbha is the highest point within the realm of *saṁsāra* that one can reach through inferior knowledge (*etadantās tu saṁsāragatayo 'parāvidyāgamyāh, Mu. Up.Bh.* 1.2.11. p. 16.24; p. 17.4.). Release and *parā vidyā,* the knowledge of the highest Brahman, are truly but one and the same thing. If it be said that knowledge is the means of release, it must be added that in this case means and end are inseparable, for knowledge unlike action carries its own fruit within itself; and moreover, within this sphere a distinction such as that of means and end amounts to no more than a mere figure of speech. But the result of lower knowledge, such as the attainment of Hiraṇyagarbha, is characterised by means and end, actions and results, and comes within the realm of duality (*Mu. Up.Bh.* 1.2.11. p. 17.7-8).

Hiraṇyagarbha Identified with Mahān Ātmā

Kaṭha Upanishad, 3.10.11 speaks of the gradation of different entities.

Beyond the senses are the objects of sense; beyond the mind the intellect; and beyond the intellect is *mahān ātmā;* beyond the *mahān ātmā* is the unmanifest (*avyakta*); beyond the unmanifest (*avyakta*) is Puruṣa. This is the end and the final goal.

Śaṃkara attempts to prove that here *mahān ātmā* means Hiraṇyagarbha. Hiraṇyagarbha is called Ātmā, because he is the internal principle of the intelligence of all living beings (*sarva-prānī-buddhīnām pratyag-ātmabhūtatvāt*). And he is called Great (*mahān*) as being the greatest of all (*Kaṭha. Up. Bh.* 3.10. p. 66.2-4).

The *Bh.G* passage (3.42) which corresponds to the Kaṭha. Up. passage quoted above reads as follows:

The senses are superior. Beyond the senses is the mind; beyond the mind is the intellect, That which is beyond the intellect is He (*yo buddheḥ paratas tu saḥ*).

Commenting on the last expression 'That which is beyond the intellect is He' (*yo buddheḥ paratas tu saḥ*), Śaṃkara says :

He who is interior to all things seen (*sarvadṛsyebhyo buddhyantebhyo bhyantara*) that dweller in the body, the individual self (*dehin*) whom it has been said, desire seated in the senses and other quarters bewilders by enveloping his wisdom, He, the seer of intellect is the Supreme Self (*paramātmā*) superior to intellect (*Bh. G. Bh.* 3.42. p. 132.27; p. 133.1-2).

This interpretation of the entity beyond the intellect as the individual self (*dehin*) is different from that in *Kaṭha.Up.Bh.* where the entity beyond the intellect is spoken of as Hiraṇya-garbha.

The interpretation of *mahān ātmā* or mahat in *Kaṭha.Up.Bh.* as Hiraṇyagarbha is to prove that the term does not mean the

Mahat of the Sāṃkhya system, the first product of Prakṛti (*cf. B.S. Bh.* 2.1.2. p. 403.13; p. 404.1-6).

'Hiraṇyagarbha Identified with Prāṇa

Śaṃkara gives different interpretation of *Prāṇa*. *Prāṇa* designates for him the metaphysical life principle of Brahman or the physical life principle of the psychic organs or the *mukhya prāṇa* in a limited sense. Besides these meanings *Prāṇa* also signifies the whole complex of the subtle body and its organs. It is the empirical life principle shaped to the complex of the subtle body. As such Prāṇa as a creation of Īśvara is called Hiraṇyagarbha (*prāṇam hiraṇyagarbhākhyam, P. Up. Bh.* 6.4. p. 67. 4-6). From Brahman is produced the unmanifested common cause (*avyākṛtam sādhāraṇam kāraṇam*). From this unmanifested cause is produced *Prāṇa,* Hiranyagarbha, the common cosmic entity (*jagat-sādhāraṇa*), endowed with the power of knowledge and activity of Brahman (*Mu. Up. Bh.* 1.1.8.p. 10.4-6). This *Prāṇa,* called Hiraṇyagarbha, the first born entity, also gives birth to Virāj (*prathamajāt prāṇāt hiraṇyagarbhāt, Mu. Up. Bh.* 2.1.4. p. 23.7).

Hiranyagarbha Identified with the Lower Brahman

In *Ait Up. Bh.* Hiraṇyagarbha is identified with the lower Brahman (*brahmā-param,* p. 81.5-6). Hiraṇyagarbha is the combination of the power of knowledge and activity of the lower Brahman (*apara-brahma-vijñāna-kriyāśakti-dvayātmakā, Kaṭha. Up. Bh.* 6.1. p. 104.5). He is also designated by the old *bhedā-bheda* term of *kāryalakṣaṇam brahma* (*Mu.Up.Bh.* 1.1.9. p. 11.6). Besides the epithet of *satya brahma* is given to Hiraṇya- garbha because of his greatness. How is he great? Because he is the projector of everything. *Satya brahma* produced Virāj, who in turn produced the gods (*B.A. Up.Bh.* 5.5.1. p. 718.7-11).

Hiraṇyagarbha Identified with Prajāpati

Hiraṇyagarbha is sometimes identified with Prajāpati. Prajāpati wishing to create the universe became Hiraṇyagarbha, and was born at the beginning of the world-cycle (*P.Up.Bh.* 1.4. p. 4.5.7). Hiraṇyagarbha is the same as Aditi. Aditi is born as Hiraṇyagarbha from the highest Brahman, in the form of all the *devatās* (*Kaṭha. Up. Bh.* 4.7. p. 82.16; p. 83.7).

Hiraṇyagarbha and Brahman, The Supreme Self

Just as the individual self from the standpoint of ultimate truth is nothing but Brahman, and it is only owing to limiting adjuncts that it retains its individuality, just so Hiraṇyagabha is in reality nothing but Brahman. Because of limiting adjuncts we speak of the transmigration of Hiraṇyagarbha and his difference from the Supreme Self (*ekatvam nānātvam ca*). On the other hand, because he possesses adjuncts of extraordinary purity, the scriptures more often speak of him as the Supreme Self, and seldom as the transmigratory self (*B.A. Up. Bh.* 1.4.6. p. 105.2-6). "The one absolute entity, Brahman, becomes Hiraṇyagarbha when characterised by the notion of self in the intelligence, which is the seed of all the manifested universe (*vyākṛtajagad-bījabhūta-buddhyātmābhimāna-lakṣaṇam*)", *Ait. Up. Bh.* 5.3.. 85.4-5). "The transcendent Supreme Self assumes the name and form of Hiraṇyagarbha when it has the limiting adjuncts of the bodies and organs of Hiraṇyagarbha," *B.A. Up. Bh.* 3.8.12 (p. 469.3-5). Like the individual self separated from the Supreme Self, Hiraṇyagarbha, with his limiting adjuncts and transmigrating nature, arises and perishes at the beginning and end of creation. Though but an individual self, he is the highest in the hierarchy within the sphere of *saṁsāra*.

Hiraṇyagarbha and Īśvara

Whereas Hiraṇyagarbha is born and dies at the beginning and end of each world creation, Īśvara outlasts all the drama of creation. Īśvara creates the universe; and as the eternal god, he is not drawn into the world. And Hiraṇyagarbha is the first creation, which then helps Īśvara in the remaining work of creation.

Himself a creature and the first-born of creation, Hiraṇyagarbha holds office at the discretion of Īśvara. The power is delegated to him by Īśvara.

Das System des Vedānta trans. by Charles Johnston, The System of the Vedānta, Chicago, The Open Court Publishing Co., 1912.

Abbreviations

All editions are of the Ānandāśrama Sanskrit Series, Poona.

Ait.Up.Bh.	:	Aitareyopaniṣad with the bhāṣya of Śamkara, No. 11, 1890,
B.A. Up. Bh.	:	Bṛhadāraṇyakopaniṣad with the bhaṣya of Śamkara, No. 15, 1891
B.S. Bh.	:	Brahmasūtra with the bhaṣya of Śaṃkara, No. 20, Part I, No. 21, Part II, 1890, 1891.
Bh. G.	:	Bhagavad Gītā.
Bh.G.Bh.	:	Bhagavadgītā with the bhāṣya of Śaṃkara, No. 34, 1897.
Īśa. Up. Bh.	:	Īśāvāsyopaniṣad with the bhāṣya of Śaṁkaram, No. 5, 1888.
Kaṭha. Up. Bh	:	Kaṭhopaniṣad with the bhāṣya of Śaṃkara, No. 9, 1889.
Mu. Up. Bh.	:	Muṇḍaka Upaniṣad with the bhāṣya of Śaṃkara, No. 9, 1889.
P.Up.Bh.	:	Praśna Upaniṣad with the bhāṣya of Śaṃkara, No. 8, 1889.
Tait. Up. Bh.	:	Taittirīyopaniṣad with the bhāṣya of Śaṃkara, No. 12, 1889.

Chapter 2

Authenticity of the Bhagavadgītābhāṣya Attributed to Śaṁkarācārya

On the basis of Sanskrit catalogues, Dr. S.K. Belvalkar in his *Vedānta Philosophy*, Part I (1929) has enumerated some four-hundred works generally attributed to the great Śaṁkarācārya. The tradition of Śaṁkara's death at the age of thirty-two makes it highly improbable that he should have been the author of so many works. Apart from the question of forgery, Dr. Paul Hacker[1] offers three explanations as to why such a large number of writings has been attributed to the great Bhāṣyakāra. The most relevant reason given is that all the *jagadgurus* of the Śṛṅgeri Maṭha, which is believed to have been founded by the great Śaṁkarācārya, have borne the title Śaṁkarācārya. So any literary work by any of these spiritual heads of the Maṭha might have come to be attributed to the famous Bhāṣyakāra Śaṁkarācārya. Again there is the possibility of anonymous texts which were used in the Maṭhas, coming to be attributed to the founder of the Maṭha. Finally there is the possibility that works of still other authors, who bore the name of Śaṁkara and who were *ācāryas*, came to be confused with the works of the great Bhāṣyakāra. Out of the huge mass of literature ascribed to the great Bhāṣyakāra many have been rejected outright by scholars as spurious. The one work which has invariably been accepted as genuine by all scholars is the commentary on the Sūtras of Bādarāyaṇa, the *Brahmasūtra-Bhāṣya*. Many writers have written commentaries and super commentaries on this particular work. Prof. S.N. Dasgupta in his *A History of Indian Philosophy,* Vol. II (1932), pp. 81-82 has given a list of commentaries and super-commentaries written on this work. This shows that it has the strength of tradition behind it to support its authenticity. In his book *Naiṣkarmyasiddhi,* Sureśvara speaks of his teacher who explained the truths of the Vedas (1.5). He obtained the truth of Vedānta from his teacher Śaṁkara (4.76). People should not be prejudiced against his work (*mā bhūd atra virodhinī matir*), because the truth explained in his book he had learnt at the feet of the great Śaṁkarācārya (*Śrīmat Śaṁkara-pāda-padma-yugalam saṁsevya*) (4. 74). Sureśvara's teacher Śaṁkara, at whose instruction he wrote the work *Naiṣkarmysiddhi* (1.3) is none other than the great Bhāṣyakāra to whose authority he appeals to save himself from criticism. Another work, the *pañcapādikā*, is a commentary on the *Brahma-Sūtra-Bhāṣya* (1. 1. 1-4). In the invocatory verse 3 of this work, its author Padmapāda bows to his teacher, the unique Śaṁkara (*apūrva Śaṁkara*). In verse 4 he bows his head before the teachers, renowned for their knowledge of the *Bhāṣya* (*bhāṣya-vittaka-gurūn*), to the Mānasa-lake of whose mouth the *Bhāṣya*-lotus owes its birth (*yadvaktra-mānasa-saraḥ pratilabdha-janma bhāṣyāravinda*). This makes us clear that Śaṁkara was the composer of the *Brahma-Sūtra-Bhāṣya*; and Padmapāda and Sureśvara were his pupils.

Śaṁkarācārya was called by his contemporaries *Bhagavat*, *Bhagavatapāda* and *Bhagavatpūjyapāda*. In *Naiṣkarmyasiddhi* (4. 19. 43), Sureśvara calls his teacher *Bhagavatpūjyapāda* or *Bhagavatpāda*. Jñānottama[2] never calls him Śaṁkara but *bhāṣyakāra, Bhagavatpāda-ācārya, Bhagavatapūjyapāda-ācārya* and *ācārya*. The *Brahma-Sūtra-Bhāṣya* is invariably ascribed to Śaṁkara-*Bhagavat, -Bhagavatpāda* or *-Bhagavatpūjyapāda* in the colophons. Dr Paul Hacker taking his stand on the colophons of the *Brahma-Sūtra-Bhāṣya* arrives at the conclusion that the works ascribed in the colophons to Śaṁkara, *-Bhagavat, -Bhagavatpāda, Bhagavatpūjyapāda* are to be taken as genuine; whereas all works containing in their colophons the simple title Śaṁkara-*ācārya* are of doubtful authority. Dr. Hacker[3] admits that the authorship problem cannot be solved by the superficial method of examining colophons. Despite the fact that colophons to

Śvetāśvataropaniṣad-Bhāṣya name the author as *Bhagavat,* on the basis of internal grounds the work must be rejected as spurious. On the basis of internal evidence, *Māṇḍūkya-Kārikā-Bhāṣya,*[4] the *Kena Upaniṣad Vākya-Bhāṣya*[5] have been regarded as spurious. The authorship of *Vivekacūḍāmaṇī*[6] with no commentary attributed to it is regarded as dubious.

Prof. S.N. Dasgupta,[7] Sarvepalli Radhakrishnan,[8] M. Hiriyanna[9] do not question Bhāṣyakāra Śaṁkara's authorship of the *Bhagavadgītā-Bhāṣya.* Prof. S.K. Belvalkar[10] regards the *Bhagavadgītā-Bhāṣya* "as most probably coming from Śaṁkarācārya himself". Barend Faddegon in his book, Śaṁkara's *Gītā-Bhāṣya* (1906) examines some of the points in the *Bhagavadgītā-Bhāṣya* and the *Brahma-Sūtra-Bhāṣya.* He asserts : "We need not doubt the identity of the authorship of *Bhāṣya* and *Gītā-Bhāṣya*" (p. 63), as "there is the continuing correspondence in the terminology, language and thought" (p. 65). Though Prof. Daniel H.H. Ingalls[11] sees no reason to doubt the ascription of the *Bhagavadgītā-Bhāṣya* to Bhāṣyakāra Śaṁkarācārya, Dr. Hacker does not believe the authenticity of the *Bhagavadgītā-Bhāṣya*, and questions the conclusions reached by Faddegon.[12]

Comparative Study of the Trend of Philosophical Thought in the Brahma-Sūtra-Bhāṣya and the Bhagavadgītā-Bhāṣya

In *Brahma-Sūtra-Bhāṣya* a question arises as to the partiality of god in the creation of the Universe. He renders the gods of heaven eminently happy; the animals eminently unhappy; and to man he allots an intermediate position. Because of this unequal distribution, one is tempted to ascribe passion and malice to god.

To these two suggestions of god's cruelty and partiality, Śaṁkara replies both as a religious realist and a subjective idealist. In *Brahma-Sūtra-Bhāṣya* (2.1.34) he absolves god from any responsibility whatsoever by making *Karma* responsible for every thing. In the creation of creatures, in the distribution of happiness and misery, god does not act arbitrarily but is bound by his regard for the good and evil works (*sāpekṣa īśvara*) of each creature done in earlier births.

Śaṁkara, in support of his theory, adduces scriptural proofs in his *Brahma-Sūtra-Bhāṣya* (2. 1. 34) from the *Bhagavadgītā*. In *Brahma-Sūtra-Bhāṣya* (2. 1. 34) he introduces a line from the *Bhagavadgītā* with these words : "*Smṛti* passages also declare the favour of the Lord and its opposite (*anugrahītṛtvam nigrahītṛtvam ca*) to depend on variation in the works of living beings (*prāṇī-karma-viśeṣāpekṣam eva*)."[13] The first line of the *Bhagavadgītā* 4. 11 quoted in the *Brahma-Sūtra-Bhāṣya* 2.1.34 is, "I serve men in the way in which they approach me."[14] Now it is interesting to examine whether the commentary of the *Bhagavadgītā* on this particular *śloka* actually expounds the concept hinted in the *Brahma-Sūtra-Bhāṣya*.

The *Bhagavadgītā-Bhāṣya*, in introducing the 11th verse of the 4th Chapter says, "Dost thou cherish feelings of affection and aversion (*rāga-dveṣau*), since thou awardest liberation to a few only, not to all?"[15] The answer is, "I serve men in the way in which they approach me."[16] Śaṁkara comments on this line:

"I bestow my grace on people by granting the things they desire, just in accordance with the way by which they seek me and the motive with which they seek me (*yat phalārthitayā*); for they do not seek for liberation. One cannot indeed pursue pleasure, and seek for liberation at the same time. Wherefore, I serve the selfish (*phalārthinaḥ*) by securing to them their selfish ends (*tat-phala-dānena*). I serve the unselfish (*aphalārthinaḥ*) who do their prescribed duties and seek for liberation by granting them knowledge. I serve the men of knowledge (*jñāninaḥ*), who have renounced the world and seek for liberation by granting liberation. I serve the distressed (*ārttān*) by relieving them from distress. Thus do I serve men just in the way they approach me. But never do I serve any from affection and aversion or from ignorance."[17]

This commentary on the *Bhagavadgītā* looks irrelevant when read in line with what the *Brahma-Sūtra-Bhāṣya* (2. 1. 34) has to say on this verse. While the *Brahma-Sūtra-Bhāṣya* (2. 1. 34) quotes the *Bhagavadgītā* line to show how the favour and disfavour of the Lord depend on the quality of works of living beings (p. 481, 16-17) the *Bhagavadgītā-Bhāṣya* shows how god bestows grace on people by granting the things they desire, depending upon their method of approach, and their motive too (*yena prayojanena*). In the *Bhagavadgītā-Bhāṣya* (4. 11) god bestows grace on people in four ways, as Śaṁkara illustrates. He secures selfish ends to the selfish. He gives knowledge to the unselfish seeking for liberation. He gives liberation to the men of knowledge. He takes away the distress from the distressed. All these instances indicate that the god is not a passive dispenser of the fruits of *Karma* but he is kind and benevolent lord ready to help everybody. When one becomes good through good work, evil through evil work (*Brahma-Sūtra-Bhāṣya* 2. 1. 34 p. 481. 15), how can we justify the action of god, as described in the *Bhagavadgītā-Bhāṣya*, in taking away the distress from the distressed? Unlike the *Brahma-Sūtra-Bhāṣya* (2. 1. 34) the *Bhagavadgītā-Bhāṣya* (4. 11) makes no mention of the responsibility of *Karma* for the misery or inequality existing in the world. Thus this difference in the trend of thought makes us doubt the authenticity of the *Bhagavadgītā-Bhāṣya* as the work of Bhāṣyakāra Śaṁkara.

Comparative Study of the Peculiar Terminologies used by Saṁkara in the Brahma-Sūtra-Bhāṣya, Bṛhad-Āraṇyaka-Upaniṣad-Bhāṣya[18] *and in the Bhagavadgītā and in the Bhagavadgītā-Bhāṣya.*

According to Śaṁkara, the most common expression with *avidyā* as the first in the series is *avidyā-kāma-karma* (ignorance-desire-action). In *Bṛhadāraṇyaka-Upaniṣad-Bhāṣya* 4.3.30, Śaṁkara explains this causal chain of *avidyā-kāma-karma.* "The nature of ignorance proves to be this, that it represents the true universal Self which is infinite as finite, brings up to it (and confuses with it) things other than the Self, which are non-existent, makes the Self appear as limited. Thence arises the desire for that which seems to be outside the Self. Desire for that from which it is separated drives it to action; and this produces consequences. The *Upadeśa Sāhasrī* (*Padya-bandha,*

1. 6-7) gives the same interpretation of the causal chain of *avidyā-kāma-karma*. This causal chain of *avidyā-kāma-karma* is a favourite of Śaṁkara, and appears with much more frequency than any other expression.

In the description of the effects of *avidyā* one comes across the following expressions :

The individual Self is brought about by ignorance (*avidyā-pratyupasthāpita*).

❑ *Brahma-Sūtra-Bhāṣya* 2. 3. 46 (p. 667. 13)

Saṁsāra is superimposed by ignorance (*avidyā- adhyāropita*).

❑ *Bṛhad-Āraṇyaka-Upaniṣad-Bhāṣya* 1.1.1. (p. 12. 5-6)

The limiting adjuncts of the body and organs are caused by ignorance (*avidyā-kalpita*)

❑ *Bṛhad-Āraṇyaka-Upaniṣad-Bhāṣya* 2. 4. 14 (p. 340. 8-9)

From the use of peculiar terminologies like *pratyupasthāpita, adhyasta, adhyāropita, vijṛmbhita, kalpita*, we know that a peculiar relation of causality between *avidyā* and its effects was in the mind of Śaṁkara.

As Dr. Hacker says in his article,[19] most scholars have made no attempt to dissociate the ideas of Śaṁkara from that of his followers like Padmapāda and Sureśvara. Dr. Hacker shows that there are many ideas which are present in a rudimentary stage in Śaṁkara, but are later elaborated by his followers. The traditional characteristic of *avidyā* is its operation in a two-fold manner, suppression (*āvaraṇa*) and projection (*vikṣepa*). This distinction is absent from Śaṁkara, unless we may read *vikṣepa* aspect of *avidyā* into the passage of the *Bṛhad-Āraṇyaka-Upaniṣad-Bhāṣya* (4. 3. 20 p. 557. 12).

In the *Bhagavadgītā-Bhāṣya*, peculiar expressions like *avidyā-adhyāropita, avidyā-kalpita, avidyā-parikalpita, avidyā-nimittaka,* besides *avidyākṛta* and *avidyātmaka* are not uncommon. In definitive terms the *Bhagavadgītā-Bhāṣya* (14. 6.

p. 413. 27-29) speaks of *avidyā* thus : Happiness has come to me. Such an attachment to happiness is but false. It is *avidyā;* because an attribute of the object cannot belong to the subject. This definition of *avidyā* agrees well with that given in Śaṁkara's other works. The causal chain of *avidyā-kāma-karma* so popular with Śaṁkara occurs three times in the *Bhagavadgītā-Bhāṣya* though expressed in different ways : *avidyā-kāma-kleśa-bīja-nimittāni hi karmāṇi* (13. 23. p. 398. 26) *avidyā-kāma-bījam hi sarvam eva karma* (18. 66. p. 529. 5). Very often Śaṁkara compares *avidyā* to defective vision '*timira dṛṣṭi.*'[20] The comparison of *avidyā* with *timira-dṛṣṭi* is carried in the *Bhagavad- gītā-Bhāṣya*—(18-48. p. 503. 6-8). As in the *Brahma-Sūtra-Bhāṣya* and the *Bṛhad-Āraṇyaka-Upaniṣad-Bhāṣya*, Śaṁkara avoids a direct answer to the question whether *avidyā* belongs to the Supreme Self or to the individual Self. The interesting discussion on the question as to whose is *avidyā* is given in *Bhagavadgītā-Bhāṣya* (13. 2. p. 371-373).

In spite of these common terminologies and common ideas, there are a few cases which make us doubt the authenticity of the *Bhagavadgītā-Bhāṣya* as written by the great Bhāṣyakāra Śaṁkara. In the *Bhagavadgītā-Bhāṣya* there are a few cases which go against our generalizations on *avidyā.* The peculiar expressions like *avidyānidrā* or *avidyāniśā* (2. 69. p. 61.16), and *avidyābhūmi* (4. 18. p. 146. 15) are uncommon with Śaṁkara. In one passage (18. 66. p. 521. 6) *avidyā* is called *anādi,* not *naisargikī* or *svābhāvikī* (*avidyā anādikāla-pravṛttā*). As in *Bṛhadāraṇyakopaniṣad-Bhāṣya* (1. 4. 17. p. 184. 8), here also (13. 2. p. 362. 2) *avidyā* is termed *āvaraṇātmikā,* partaking of the nature of a veil. But the explicit definition of the three forms of *avidyā* (*avidyā-traya* 13. 2. p. 362. 2-3) causing perception of what is quite the contrary of truth (*viparīta-grāhaka*), or causing doubt (*saṁśayopasthāpaka*) or causing non-perception of a truth (*agrahaṇātmaka*) seems to be the later expounded version of *avidyā.* Then there is the definition of *avidyā* as *Puruṣa* seated in *Prakṛti* (*prakṛtisthatvākhyā avidyā,* 13. 21. p. 395. 7), which seems a bit strange in Śaṁkara's description of *avidyā.*

References

1. 'Saṁkarācārya and Śaṁkarabhagavatpāda.' *New Indian Antiquary,* Vol. IX, Nos. 4-6 April-June, 1947, pp. 1-2.
2. Referred to by Dr. Paul Hacker, *Untersuchungen über Texte frühen Avaitavāda,* p. 15, Notes 2.
3. *New Indian Antiquary,* Vol. IX, Nos. 4-6. April-June, 1947, p. 9.
4. Objections to Bhāṣyakāra's authorship of the M.K. Bh. are cited by Vidhushekhara Bhattacharya, *The Āgamaśāstra of Gauḍapāda,* 1943, Introduction, p. xxxiii Notes.
5. Vidhushekhara Bhattacharya. 'Śaṁkara's commentary on the Upaniṣads', *Mookerjee Jubilee. Volume III* (part II), p. 101.
6. S.K. Belvalkar. *Vedānta philosophy,* part I (1929), p. 228. Notes.
7. *A History of Indian Philosophy* Vol. II, 1932, pp. 79-80
8. *Indian Philosophy,* Vol. II, 1929, p. 450.
9. *Outlines of Indian Philosophy,* 1932, p. 340.
10. *Op. Cit.* p. 218.
11. *Philosophy East and West,* Vol. III, No. I, April, 1953, p. 71.
12. ZDMG. Band 100, Heft I, 1956, p. 246.
13. *Brahma-Sūtra-Bhāṣya* (2. 1. 34), p. 481, 16-17.
14. *Brahma-Sūtra-Bhāṣya* 2. 1. 34. p. 482. 1.
15. *Bhagavadgītā-Bhāṣya* 4. 11. p. 140. 11-12.
16. *Bhagavadgītā Text.* 4. 11.
17. *Bhagavadgītā-Bhāṣya* 4. 11. p. 140. 15-21.
18. Bhāṣyakāra Śaṁkarā's authorship of this work is proved to be definite by Kathe Marschner in her dissertation in the University of Breslaw, *Zur Verfasserfrage Des Dem Śaṁkarācārya Zugeschriebenen-Bṛhadāraṇyakopaniṣad Bhāṣya,* 1933.
19. *ZDMG.* Band—100. Haft 1. 1950.
20. *Bṛhad-Āraṇyaka-Upaniṣhad-Bhāṣya* 1. 4. 10. p. 165. 9-11.

Bibliography

Belvalkar, S.K. *Vedanta Philosophy* (Part I), 1929.

Bhattacharya, Vidushekhara. *The Āgamaśāstra of Gauḍapāda,* 1943.

Brahmasūtra-Bhāṣya. Ānandāśrama Sanskrit Series No. 20, Pt. I, 1890; No. 21, Pt. II, 1891.

Bhagavadgītā-Bhāṣya. Ānandāśrama Sanskrit Series No. 34, 1897.

Bṛhadāraṇyakopaniṣad-Bhāṣya. *Ānandāśrama Sanskrit Series,* No. 15, 1891.

Dasgupta, S.N. *A History of Indian Philosophy* (Vol. II), 1932.

Hacker, Paul. *Untersuchungen über Texte des frühem Advaitavāda.*

Hiriyanna, M. *Outlines of Indian Philosophy*. London : George Allen & Unwin, 1932.

Radhakrishnan, S. *Indian Philosophy*. London : George Allen & Unwin, 1929.

Chapter 3

Śaṁkara's Attitude Towards the Accounts of Creation

Ācārya Śaṁkara is famous for his monumental commentaries on the Brahma-Sūtra of Bādarāyaṇa, the Upaniṣads and the Bhagavad-Gītā. The Bhagavad Gītā, the original text of the Brahma-Sūtra and the Upaniṣads contain different accounts as to the method and manner of the creation of this universe. An attempt is made in this paper to show as to how does Śaṁkara treat of these stories of creation, while commenting on these works.

Śaṁkara is primarily a theologian. His main interest lies in bringing salvation to people in the tormented world. This salvation, the realisation of Self, constitutes our ultimate purpose according to Śaṁkara. Commenting on the famous dialogue between Yājñavalkya and Maitreyī in the *Bṛhad Āraṇyaka Upaniṣad* Śaṁkara says that the object like husband, wife and wealth are not, in the last instance, loved for their own sake but for the sake of the Self. Now, if a thing is good for something else, it is that something which constitutes its true end; and since everything in the world is stated here to acquire its worth by reference to the Self, the Self must be the object of ultimate value (*tasmād ātma-prīti-sādhanatvāt gauny anyatra-prītir ātmany eva mukhyā.*) Therefore, one should realise the Self through hearing, reflection and meditation (*Bṛhad Āraṇyaka Upaniṣad Bhāṣya, 2.4.5,* p. 325. *10-13*).

So, for Śaṁkara the realisation of the Self is of ultimate value (Brāhmāvagatir hi puruṣārthaḥ, *Brahma-Sūtra Bhāṣya,* 1.1.1, p. 26. 9-10). For this reason alone he proclaims his brahmajijñāṣā. For this reason alone he spends himself in thought, and creates his doctrine and attempts to destroy opposing doctrines. 'Thus there are various opinions, some based on sound arguments and scrtiptural texts, some on fallacious arguments and scriptural texts misunderstood. If, therefore, a man would embrace some one of these opinions without previous consideration, he would bar himself from the highest beatitude, and incur grievous loss. For this reason the first Sūtra proposes, under the designation of an inquiry into Brahman, a disquisition on the Vedānta texts, to be carried on with the help of conformable arguments, and having for its aim the highest beatitude' (Brahma- Sūtra Bhāṣya, 1.1.1, p. 29.4-6, p. 30.1-2).

And what is the means for the attainment of the highest beatitude, the realisation of Self? As the story of Yājñyavalkya makes clear, it is absolute detachment from this world. So Śaṁkara pictures this world as full of horror and misery. '*Saṁsāra* is a great ocean, having for its waters the miseries resulting from ignorance, desire and action, full of the crocodiles of chronic disease, old age and death' (*Aitareya Upaniṣad Bhāṣya,* 2.1. p. 33.4-5). 'This tree of *saṁsāra* consists in manifold misery of birth, decay, death and grief' (*Kaṭha Upaniṣad Bhāṣya,* 6.1, p. 103.6-8). This picture of the world as full of pain and misery results from Śaṁkara's attempt to turn the attention of people to his ultimate value, to the realisation of the Self. So this world must be pictured as something to be discarded, hated and frowned upon. One must try to escape from the fetters of *saṁsāra* (*Saṁsāra-pāśa*), as a hawk bursts through a net, (*Aitareya Upaniṣad Bhāṣya* 4.5. p. 72.7-8). One who has fallen into this great ocean of *saṁsāra* should try to reach the shore of salvation (*mokṣa-tīra*), furnished with the raft of knowledge (*jñānoḍupa, Aitareya Upaniṣad Bhāṣya,* 2.1, p. 34. 2-3). A man in *saṁsāra* is like the man from Gāndhara who had lost his way. But because he was intelligent, he asked the right way to the next village. Thus by making his way from village to village and helped by the instructions of those he questioned, he came home at last to the people of Gāndhara. So also the man in *saṁsāra* is carried away by thieves in the shape of virtue, vice, etc., from the

Existent (*Sat*), the Self of the universe, into the forest of the body, consisting of fire, water and food, filled with wind, bile, phlegm, blood, fat, flesh, bone, marrow etc., and full of all sorts of pairs of opposites, like heat and cold, fastened by the noose of longing for a wife, son, friend, cattle, relatives and other visible and invisible objects of sense (*....aneka-viṣaya-tṛṣṇā-pāśitah*). He cries out caught in a hundredfold net (*aneka-śatasahasra-anartha-jālavān*). Then he meets one who has realised Brahman, who is free from bondage and truly blessed. This man teaches the wanderer the way to knowledge, and the failure of worldly things in the words, 'You are not of the world; the son, etc. do not belong to you. You are the Existent (*Sat*). Thou art that' (*nāsitvam saṁsārī, amuṣya putratvādi dharmavān; kim tarhi? sat yat tvam asi*). Then with his bondage of illusion removed he reaches the true Self, full of joy and peace like the man from Gāndhāra reaching his own home again. (*Chāndogya Upaniṣad Bhāṣya*, 6.14.1-2, p. 349, 354). This is how Śaṁkara analyses the Upaniṣadic story of a man lost in the misery of the world, yet longing to return home to eternal salvation. 'This is a moving passage' says Rudolf Otto (*Mysticism East and West*, p. 190). 'The cold and abstract thinker Śaṁkara here throws aside the mantle of a scholar. The heart that beats beneath his lifeless formulae throbs audibly, and in a flow of living emotion, the inner meaning of his whole speculative system breaks forth: a passionate search for salvation, for a good outside this miserable world, a homesickness, a thirst for eternity.' Thus Śaṁkara's primary motive being salvation in the realisation of the Supreme Self, he seeks a way of escape from this world of misery and woe. In accordance with this is his use of expressions like saṁsāra-pāśa, -bandhana, -jālasamudra. He seeks how this world is to be overcome and not how it is to be explained. Not being a metaphysician at heart, he was disinterested in the nature of the phenomenal universe. His accounts of creation are meant for teaching the knowledge of Brahman.

In explaining the ancient religious texts Śaṁkara has to deal with the whole of early cosmological speculation. It is only because of necessity, because of his adherence to the authority of the scriptures that he deals with the theories of creation. Otherwise the stories of creation are really of no interest to him. This point of view can be illustrated from a number of cases. In the Upaniṣadic accounts of creation one notices a discrepancy. One text reads, 'It created fire'. Another reads, 'From the Self was produced ether, from ether air, and from air fire, fire being the third in order of creation'. Śaṁkara reconciles this discrepancy by saying: (1) It is no fault. It can be assumed that the Existent (*Sat*) created fire, after having created ether and air. (2) The fact may be that the text has no eye to the order of creation. (3) It may be that what is aimed at is an exposition of trivṛt-karaṇa (*Chāndogya Upaniṣad Bhāṣya,* 6. 2. 3, p 306. 7-13). In another passage Śaṁkara returns to the question of the same discrepancy. Here again he offers three explanations: (1) The conflict of statements concerning the creation of the world does not affect the statement concerning the cause-Brahman. (2) The teacher will reconcile these conflicting statements later on. (3) The conflict of statements regarding the creation of the world does not matter greatly, since the creation of the world and similar topics are not at all what scripture wishes to teach (*bhaved api kāryasya vigītatvam apratipādyatvāt*). Continuing this last argument Śaṁkara says :

> We neither observe nor are told by scripture that the welfare of man depends upon those matters in any way. Nor have we the right to assume such a thing; because we conclude from the introductory and concluding clauses that the passages about the creation and the like form only subordinate members of passages treating of Brahman, that all the passages setting forth the creation and so on subserve the purpose of teaching Brahman. By means of comparisons such as that of the clay, creation is described merely for the purpose of teaching us that the effect is not really different from the cause (*Brahma-Sūtra Bhāṣya,* 1. 4.14 p. 363. 8-16).

In another place of the same text Śaṁkara discusses the question and comes to the conclusion that the creation stories are insignificant. The opponent says that those passages which state the origin of the world cannot be understood to teach anything but just the creation of the world. To this Śaṁkara replies that the texts by means of the simile of the lump of clay, etc. teach that only Brahman is true and everything else is untrue; they do not aim at teaching the creation of the world. The opponent says: But why should passages about the creation of the world be subordinate to those which deny any difference and not vice versa? To this Śaṁkara answers that the texts which negative all difference, effect the cessation of desire. Once the absolute unity of the Self has been apprehended, the highest aim of man is attained, and, therefore, there is an end of desire. Texts speaking of the creation of the world have no similar power of effecting the cessation of all desire. Passages about creation aim at teaching the unity of the Self (*Brahma-Sūtra Bhāṣya 4.3.14,* p. 1116.4; p. 1117.10). Passages delineating the origin, continuity and dissolution of the universe are for strengthening the idea of the identity of the individual Self with the supreme Self (*Bṛhad Āraṇyaka Upaniṣad Bhāṣya, 1.4.7,* p. 119. 16-17; p. 120.11-12; 2.1.20, p. 280.7-8; p. 282.5-6). The Self has been ascertained to be homogeneous unborn consciousness, like a lump of salt. Scripture does not wish to teach that, like a painted canvas, a tree or an ocean, Brahman has diverse attributes such as the origin of the universe. 'It should be realised in one form only'. 'He goes from death to death who sees difference, as it were, in it'. All these statements show that 'the mention in all Vedānta texts of the origin, continuity and dissolution of the universe is only to strengthen our idea of Brahman being a homogeneous unity and not to make us believe in the origin, etc., as an actuality' (*Bṛhad Āraṇyaka Upaniṣad Bhāṣya, 2.1.20,* p. 282. 1-6). In order to inculcate a knowledge of the nature of Brahman we have shown the effect of it, beginning with ether and ending with food' (*Taittirīya Upaniṣad Bhāṣya, 2.6*, p. 66.16; p. 67.2). The scriptural doctrine of creation aims at intimating that Brahman is the Self of everything (*brahmātma-bhāva-pratipādana-paratvāt, Bramha Sūtra Bhāṣya, 2.1.33,* p. 479. 10-12). The scriptures describe changes or modifications, only for the purpose of the knowledge of the absolute entity through them (*Bramha Sūtra Bhāṣya*, 2. 1. 27, p. 472. 8-11). To explain the nature of numbers from one upto a hundred thousand billions, one superimposes them on certain lines, calling the number in the last column one, that in the preceding column ten, in the preceding column one hundred and so on. Thus one expounds the nature of numbers (*avagamayati saṁkhyā-svarūpam kevalam*), but one never says that the numbers are the lines (*na tu saṁkhyāyāḥ rekhātmatvam eva).* In order to teach the alphabet one has recourse to a combination of leaf, ink, lines, etc., and through them one explains the nature of the letters; but one never says that the letters are the leaf, ink, etc.; similarly the one entity Brahman has been inculcated through various means such as creation, etc. (u*tpattyādy anekopāyam āsthāya ekam brahmatattvam āveditam, Bṛhad-Āraṇyaka Upaniṣad Bhāṣya, 4.4.24*, p. 674.9-15).

Thus for Śaṁkara the accounts of creation are insignificant (*utpattiśruti gauṇī, Brahma-Sūtra Bhāṣya, 2.3.3,* p. 590.3-4). They are for him only a means for the attainment of the ultimate truth. Śaṁkara even goes to the extent of branding them as false. Besides the method of his reconciling the discrepancies in the accounts of creation, his explicit statements about the stories of creation leave no doubt that his interest in the universe is derived and secondary. Śaṁkara's chief interest being the mystical union of Brahman and Ātman, he does not care to discover how the universe works. He gives rough and incomplete answers to questions of Avidyā. The relation between the Supreme Brahman and the empirical universe, he expresses through the concept of *māyā,* 'in itself a recognition of the inexplicability of the world and a depreciation of its value'. (*W.S. Urquhart, The Vedānta and Modern Thought,* p. 148). In a way Śaṁkara's concept of *avidyā* and *māyā* covers up his confusion, and leaves many questions unsolved. Radhakrishnan best expresses the attitude of Śaṁkara towards the universe: 'As for the empirical ramifications which also exist, well, they are there; and there is an end of it. We do not know how and cannot know why. It is all a contradiction; and yet it is actual'. (*S. Radhakrishnan, Indian Philosophy,* Vol. I, p. 35).

Books Referred to

1. *Aitareyopaniṣad* with the Bhāṣya of Śaṁkara, Ānandāśrama Sanskrit series, No. 11, 1890.
2. *Brahma-Sūtra Bhāṣya, Ānandāśrama* Sanskrit Series, No. 20, 1890 and No. 21, 1891.
3. *Bṛhad-Āraṇyaka Upaniṣad* with the Bhāṣya of Śaṁkara, Ānandāśrama Sanskrit Series, No. 15, 1891.
4. Chāndogya Upaniṣad with the Bhāṣya of Śaṁkara, Ānandāśrama Sanskrit Series, No. 14, 1890.
5. Kaṭha Upaniṣad with the Bhāsya of Śaṁkara, Ānandāśrama Sanskrit Series, No. 7, 1889.
6. Taittirīyopaniṣad with the Bhāsya of Śaṁkara, Ānandāśrama Sanskrit Series, No. 12, 1889.

CHAPTER 4

Concept of Lakṣmī and Sarasvatī in the Later Upaniṣads

The later Upaniṣads are on the whole sectarian in character. The worship of the five deities-Viṣṇu, Śiva, Devī, Sūrya and Gaṇesa, which is the characteristic feature of the post-Vedic Aryan religion, is dealt with in great detail in these Upaniṣads. These Upaniṣads which emphasise the importance of Devī are known as Śākta Upaniṣads. In these Śākta Upaniṣads Devī in her various forms as Kālī, Śakti, Lakṣmī, Sarasvatī and Vanadurgā, is raised to the position of the highest self. These Upaniṣads, therefore, state that the other gods are subordinate to Devī. The goddesses which are the various forms of Devī are again divided into two classes, one belonging to Śiva and the other to Viṣṇu. These two classes do not clash against each other; but they are said to be complementary to both these great gods. The Saivite deities however exhibit two distinct traits of character as mild and awful. If Kāli and Tripurā are awful, Uma is mild in her character. Durgā presents a combined form, rather a cosmic form and absorbs in her personality all the other deities. The Vaisnavite goddesses like Tulasī, Rādhā, Sarasvatī, Sāvitrī, Lakṣmī and Sītā are not dreadful in their character, and present a more delicate and charming personality.

There are twenty-seven Upaniṣads devoted to Devī. They are as follows:

1. Atharvanadvitiyopaniṣad,
2. Kāmarājakīlakopaniṣad,
3. Kālikopaniṣad,

4. Kālimedhādīkṣitopaniṣad,
5. Gayatrīrahasyopaniṣad,
6. Gāyatryupaniṣad,
7. Guhyakālyupaniṣad,
8. Guhyasodhānyāsopaniṣad,
9. Tripuropaniṣad,
10. Tripurātāpinyupaniṣad,
11. Devyupaniṣad,
12. Pītāmbaropaniṣad,
13. Bahvṛcopaniṣad,
14. Bhāvanopaniṣad,
15. Rājasyāmalārahasyopaniṣad,
16. Vanadurgopaniṣad,
17. Syāmopaniṣad,
18. Srīcakropaniṣad,
19. Srīvidyātārakopaniṣad,
20. Srīrādhikātāpinyupaniṣad,
21. Srirādhopaniṣad,
22. Sodhopaniṣad,
23. Sarasvatīrahasyopaniṣad,
24. Sītopaniṣad,
25. Sumukhyupaniṣad,
26. Saubhāgyalakṣmyupaniṣad,
27. Haiṃsāsoḍhopaniṣad.

Out of these twenty-seven Upanisads, only three, that is, Nos. 9,13 and 26 belong to the Rig-Veda, and the rest twenty-four belong to the Atharva-Veda. It can thus be seen that almost all the Upaniṣads devoted to Devī belong to the Atharva-Veda by tradition. The doctrines depicted here may be said to be Atharvanic in character.

Personality and Description of Devī

Devī dwells in the midst of the lotus of the heart. Her complexion is like that of the rising sun. She holds the noose and goad, a bow and arrows in her hands. Her form is attractive. She forms *Varadā* and *Abhayā* mudrās by her hands. She has three eyes. She wears red clothes. She is *Ajñeya* (difficult to know) and *Ananta* (endless). Her form is invisible. She is devoid of birth and death. She is omnipresent and so is called *Ekā*. Though one, she is seen in many forms; so she is *Naikā*. Devī dwells in all the spells as the *Mātṛkā* (the original syllable), and as the meaning in the words. She is known as Durgā also.

The associates of Devī are not mentioned because she is here praised as the Highest Self. She is the Creator of all. Devī in her other forms has been described to have a family. The exploits of Devī in general are enumerated here. She destroys sins, kills demons, creates, maintains and destroys the universe. Devī is *Aparā Śakti,* The three cities of Devī are then identified with various groups of three things. The nineteen names of Devī are described in the Bahvṛcopaniṣad as follows : (1) Bālā (2) Ambikā, (3) Bagalā, (4) Mātaṅgi (5) Svayambarā kalyāṇī, (6) Bhuvaneśvarī, (7) Cāmuṇḍā, (8) Caṇḍa, (9) Vārāhī, (10) Tiraskariṇī, (11) Rājamātaṅgī, (12) Śukaśyāmalā, (13) Laghusyāmalā, (14) Aśvārūḍhā, (15) Pratyaṇgirā, (16) Dhūmavatī, (17) Sāvitrī (18) Sarasvatī and (19) Brahmāṇḍakalā. Devī or Śakti is identifed with the Ṛcs which are placed in the highest heaven. This highest heaven is the world of *Brāhman,* which is residence of Devī. Devī is identified with the Vidyās like Sāmbhavī, Kādi, Hādi and Sādi.

The method of worshipping Devī forms the muttering of spells-Vedic and tantric, the adoration of various diagrams and Cakras like Srīcakra. The fruit according to the lower type of worship is worldly; but the higher type of worship leads one to union with the Goddess who is the *Brahman* incarnate. Devī is described as (*i*) Annapūrṇā, (*ii*) Umā (Pārvatī or Gaurī), (*iii*) Kālī, (*iv*) Gāyatrī, (*v*) Tulasī, (*vi*) Tripurā, (*vii*) Durgā, (*viii*) Pītāmbarā, (*ix*) Rādhā, (*x*) Rājaśyāmalā, (*xi*) Śrī, (*xii*) Sarasvatī, (*xiii*) Sāvitrī, (*xiv*) Sītā, (*xv*) Sumukhī and (*xvi*) Saubhāgya Lakṣmī in the later Upaniṣads.

An attempt is made in this paper to present the concept of Lakṣmī and Sarasvatī, the two predominant forms of Devī, as they are presented in these Atharvanic Upaniṣads.

Śrī Saubhāgyalakṣmī and Lakṣmī

Śrī is described as the Goddess of beauty. Lakṣmī is referred to in the *Śatapatha Brāhmaṇa* (11.4.3), where a story is related about her. Gods proposed to Prajāpati that they should be allowed to kill Lakṣmī and appropriate her gifts. Prajāpati objected to their killing her because of her being a female, but asked the gods to take her gifts without killing her. Then Agni took from her food, Soma kingly authority, Varuṇa imperial authority, Mitra martial energy, Indra force, Bṛhaspati priestly glory, Savitṛ dominion, Pūṣana splendour, and Sarasvatī nourishment. This story perhaps prepares the background of the greatness of Devī praised in the later times. A more general name for Lakṣmī is Śrī Lakṣmī. She is the active energy or Śaktī of Viṣṇu, a Goddess of exceptional charm and beauty. She followed Viṣṇu in almost all his incarnations. When Viṣṇu became a dwarf, Lakṣmī appeared from the lotus as Padmā; when he was born as Rāma, she was Sītā; when he was Kṛṣṇa, she was Rukmiṇī. Lakṣmī is the Goddesses of Beauty, Prosperity and Fortune.

The wife of Viṣṇu is Lakṣmī or Śrī (*Rāmāyaṇa*-1,77,30) who rose from ocean, clothed in white and for whom gods and demons contended (*Rāmāyaṇa*-1.18.35). She is Fortune, as happiness and wealth; as Krishna's wife she is Rukmiṇī (*Mahābhārata* 1.61.44, 67,156) mother of Pradyumna. Lakṣmī is the sister of Dhātṛ and Vidhātṛ and mother of the sky-studs (*Mahābhārata* 1,66,50). It is a late epic trait to make her exclusively Viṣṇu's wife. Śrī beautifies Viṣṇu (*Rāmāyaṇa* 2.118,20). The *Viṣṇu*

Purāṇa gives the reason for Lakṣmī's birth. The gods were advised by Viṣṇu to churn the milky ocean, if they wanted to get freed from the curse of Durvāsas. When she came out from the milky ocean, the sages were enraptured, the heavenly singers sang her praises, and the celestial nymphs danced before her. The heavenly ele- phants poured the pure water of the rivers upon her. The sea of milk presented her with a wreath of unfading flowers; and the artists of the gods decorated her with lovely ornaments. Thus bathed, attired and adorned she cast herself on the lap of Viṣṇu, and then presented to the gods the divine cup of nectar. Indra thereby was free from the curse of Durvāsas. Lakṣmī is generally associated with Nārāyaṇa whose feet are shampooed by her when he is reclining in profound peace on the thousand-headed serpent Śeṣa in the milky ocean. When Viṣṇu incarnated as Rāma, Lakṣmī sprang of her own will from the furrow as Śītā. The *Viṣṇu Purāṇa* describes Śrī as follows: Śrī, the bride of Viṣṇu, the mother of the world, is eternal, imperishable. As he is all pervading, so she is omni-present. If Kṛṣṇa is meaning, she is speech; if he is polity, she is prudence. If he is understanding, she is intellect. If he is righteousness, she is devotion. In a word Viṣṇu is all that is called male and Lakṣ mī all that is termed female; there is nothing else than these two.

Lakṣmī or Saubhāgya-Lakṣmī in the Later Upaniṣads

The Mūlaprakṛti Lakṣmī is the Siddha Lakṣmī of the Siddhas, and she can be pleased by the seven-syllabled spell "Śrī Mahālakṣmyai namaḥ". She is Mahāsaubhāgyadāyinī, the one who bestows great splendours, the one who tempts all the world, the one of the forms of all Vidyās, the great lore, the mother of the universe, bestower of liberation on the sages, the destroyer of the demons and the giver of knowledge. That is why she is addressed along with Nārāyaṇa giving the first place in the address as Lakṣmī-Nārāyaṇa. Lakṣmī is the Mahāmāyā of supreme *Brahman* in the form of the revered Nārāyaṇa. She is Devalakṣmī of gods, Siddhalakṣmī of the Siddhas, Mokṣalakṣmī of Mumukṣus, Yogalakṣmī of Yogins, Vivekabuddhi of the sages, and Rājalakṣmī of kings. The act of creation is ascribed to

Lakṣmī as Sarasvatī, that of maintenance to Mahālakṣmī, the one of destruction to her form as Rudrāṇī, the one of becoming invisible (tirodhāna) to Pārvatī and that of favouring or blessing the world (Anugraha) to Umā. Mahālakṣmī is the Prakṛti, who bestows great glory and splendours on beings and attracts all the world. She is of the form of all Vedas. She is the Mulaprakṛti; so these are together called as Lakṣmīnārāyaṇa by the Vaiṣṇavas (*Nārāyaṇa-Pūrva-tāpinī-Upaniṣad-2*). Lakṣmī represents one of the two duties with Nārāyaṇa representing the *Ūrdhvapuṇḍra* (*Nārada Upaniṣad*). Lakṣmī worshipped the Śiva-liṅga of subtle form (*Siddhāntaśikhā Upaniṣad*). Lakṣmī, the daughter of the milky ocean is the mistress of *Śrīraṅgadhāma.* She reduced to servitude the beloveds of all gods. She wins over Brahmā, Indra and Gaṅgāḍhara by her loving glance. She is born in a lotus and is the beloved of Mukunda. The *Lakṣmī Gāyatrī is given as :*

> *"Mahādevyai ca Vidmahe, Viṣṇupatnyai ca dhīmahi, Tanno Laksmīḥ pracodayāt" (Vanadurgā Upaniṣad)*

Saubhāgyalakṣmī has four arms. She is of golden complexion. She is of the form of Turiyā or even beyond that. She has the spells for her seat, and is encircled by the deities of Pīṭha and Upapītha. Śrī Mahā Lakṣmī is seated on the petal of a red lotus. Her complexion is yellow. She holds a *Varadā mudrā* by one hand, *Abhayā-mudrā* by the other, and a lotus in each of the other two hands. She possesses unique beauty, which is enhanced by jewelled bracelets and various ornaments. This mother of all endows the devotees with glory. *Śrī sūkta* is explained with reference to Lakṣmī. The one syllabled spell of this Goddess is "Śrīḥ". Two white elephants sprinkle water over her, through the pitchers held in their trunks. Her head is adorned with a crown studded with gems and diamonds. Her attire is white; her limbs are besmeared with sandal-wood paste etc., according to their respective seasons. The lotus-eyed Devī dwells on the bosom of the illustrious Viṣṇu. The author of the *Saubhāgya-Lakṣmī Upaniṣad* makes a special reference to the action without selfishness, and says that the devotee worshipping without desires alone succeeds in the *Śrīvidyā*. The thirty-two *śaktis* with reference to Saubhāgyalakṣmī are : (1) Śrī, (2) Lakṣmī, (3) Varadā, (4) Viṣṇupatnī, (5) Vasupradā, (6) Hiraṇyarūpā, (7) Svarṇamālinī, (8) Rajatasrajā, (9) Svarṇaprabhā, (10) Svarṇaprakārā, (11) Padmavāsinī, (12) Padmahastā, (13) Padmapriyā (14) Muktālaṁkārā, (15) Candrasūryā, (16) Bilvapriyā, (17) Īsvarī, (18) Bhukti, (19) Mukti, (20) Vibhūti, (21) Riddhi, (23) Kṛṣṭi, (24) Puṣṭi, (25) Dhanadā, and eight others. These adjectives speak for the auspicious character of Lakṣmī.

Sarasvatī

Sarasvatī holds an important place right from the Vedic days. She is more a river personified than a goddess with a definite form in the Rig Veda. Vāc (personified speech) is praised in one hymn of the Rig Veda (10.125). Her place is in the waters on the sea. In another passage (Rig Veda 8.89.10-11) she is called the queen of the gods and divine in her character. The later Upaniṣads have combined Sarasvatī and *Vāc* into one. Sarasvatī is invoked to grant progeny and sweetness in speech. She is described as a river also in the *Atharva Veda* (6.30.1). *Medhā* who is later on identified with Sarasvatī, is in the *Atharva Veda* (6.108.1), the personification of wisdom. *Medhā* comes to the seer with cows, horses and the rays of the sun. She is holy. She in invoked to enter into the body of the sun (*Atharva Veda* 6.208.3-5) *Vāc* and *Brahmāṇi* are the other names of Sarasvatī. The word Sarasvatī literally means the watery one. It is the ancient name of a river in the Punjab, on whose banks solemn sacrifices were performed to the gods in early times. The flow of its purifying waters was compared aptly enough to the role of eloquent speech, and music rhythm of the repetition of sacred texts and prayers. Hence Sarasvatī takes her place as the inspirer of speech, the patroness of science and literature. In later mythology Sarasvatī became under different names the wife of *Brahmā.*

According to *Manusmṛti* (4.5.92), the last watch of the night is sacred to Sarasvatī. The householder is asked to be awake in the time sacred to Sarasvatī, reflect on virtue and engaged in virtuous employment.

She is represented as a fair young woman with four arms. With one of the right hands she presents a flower to her husband; in another she holds a book of palm leaves indicating that she is the goddess of learning. In one of her left hands she has a string of pearls, and in the other a *damaru* or a small drum. She is sometimes represented as having two arms only, and as seated on a lotus, playing on the lute. She dwells amongst men but her real abode is the *Brahma-loka*.

Sarasvatī in the Later Upaniṣads

Sarasvatī is described in the *Sarasvatīrahasya Upaniṣad.* She is described as the daughter of the four-faced Brahmā. She is supremely fair, has red lips, and has her body fully adorned with ornaments. She has four hands in which she holds the *Akṣamālā*, book and weapons. She is the Goddess of speech, and is faith, retentive power and the intellect incarnate. The Upaniṣad describes her as the wife of the Creator. It appears that Prajāpati being many, the confusion of describing Sarasvatī as a wife of Brahmā might have taken place. Bramhā and Prajāpati are sometimes differently treated, and therefore it seems probable that Prajāpati married the daughter of Brahmā. In this connection the reference from the *Mahābhārata* (5.117.14) will be more instructive, where Sarasvatī is said to be the wife of Manu. The *Mahābhārata* (12.343.75) mentions Sarasvatī as the daughter of Brahmā in clear terms. So it appears that it will be in the fitness of things to take Sarasvatī as the daughter of Brahmā and not as his wife. The reference to his best for his own daughter referred to in the Śivamahimna-stotra (22) would also then be justified. Bāṇa also refers to Sarasvatī as the daughter of Brahmā in his *Harṣa-carita(i).* Sarasvatī dwells in Kashmir as well as on the tip of her devotee's tongue. She is the Goddess of poetry. Her hairs are rendered beautiful by the rays of the moon, the lord of light. She is the river of nectar that removes the distress of the worldly existence. She is indeed the *Brahman*, and hence has that Brahmanic nature. She creates the world by means of *Prakṛti*, but is in fact, *Puruṣa,* the supreme person.

Sarasvatī is the form of Lakṣmī (Sṛṣṭirūpā-sarasvatī) who is of the nature of a creation *(Nārāyaṇa-pūrva-tāpinī-Upaniṣad)*. Sarasvatī as Gāyatrī rules the western direction. She is considered to be black in complexion. She mounts an eagle, which belongs to Viṣṇu. She is the Gāyatrī in the evening. She is the ancient one and wears black garments. She has a conch shell, a discus, mace and the Abhayā Mudrā in her hands. She has Viṣṇu as her deity. She is established in the heaven. She is *Sūryarūpā*. The *Daskṣiṇāgni, Sāma Veda,* the *Vyāhṛti Svāḥ,* the third libation, the *suṣupti* condition, the *Āditya,* the *Jagati* meter, *Kriyā, Śakti, Virāj* and *Brahman* belong to her (Gāyatrī Upaniṣad). Sarasvatī is Devī Vās (*Devī Upaniṣad*) Sarasvati is the one *Śakti* of the *Brahman* (*Brahmopaniṣad*). Sacrifice is upheld by Sarasvatī. She directs sweet and truthful speech. *Medhā* is a name of Sarasvatī.

Sarasvati is sometimes treated as white in complexion also. She is adorned with *campaka* flowers, and has plump and elevated breasts. Her description is given in the ten verses (Daśa-Ślokī) in the *Sarasvatī-rahasya Upaniṣad.* She comes to the sacrifice from the luminious *Dyuloka* and goes through the clouds as big as mountains. She is beginningless and endless. She purifies all people. She is full of food. She is the inner self of all. Her waters are unfathomable. She pervades every place in the form of knowledge. She is four types of speech : *Parā, Paśyantī, madhyamā,* and *Vaikharī.* She reveals her secrets without any reserve to her devotees in the manner of a loving wife. She is the greatest amongst the mothers and the rivers. She has a royal swan as her vehicle. She sports in the Mānasa lake in the form of the mind of her devotees. Sarasvatī is liked by Brahmā. She is threefold in the forms such as *Śraddhā, Dhāraṇā* and *Medhā,* and she bestows the qualities of Sāma and *Dāna.* She is Bhavānī. She blesses the devotee with poetical powers, fearlessness and liberation if worshipped with faith, within a period of only six months.

The *Sāmavedarahasya Upaniṣad* describes that Sarasvatī serves the Rāsamaṇḍala of Rasikānanda by assuming the form of a Kalahaṃsī. Sarasvatī is referred to as the daughter of Brahmā.

She worshipped Nārāyaṇa, and then she was shown that *Līlā-Vaikuṭha*. She bathed iṇ the *Acchoda lake,* and then was allowed to enjoy all sports in the form of a royal swan in the *Vṛndāvana* and *Kāma Vana*. A Yogin becomes Sarasvatī, with the form of the syllable *Ma* (in the Oṃkāra). Sarasvatī has a bull as her vehicle. She is advanced in age and dark in complexion. She holds a trident in her hand (*Śāṇḍilya Upaniṣad*).

CHAPTER 5

Concept of Haṁsa* in the Upaniṣadic Literature

The melodious voice of swans had a great appeal for the Ṛgvedic seers. We find Bṛhaspati surrounded by his friends who cried with swan-like voices (*haṁsairiva sakhibhiḥ, vāvadadbhiḥ Ṛgveda* 10.67.3). Again we hear of Viśvāmitra, who advises the seers to sing the ślokas like swans (*haṁsāiva kṛṇutha ślokam, Ṛgveda*, 3.53.10). Because of their sweet musical note the singers who are descendants of Vṛṣagaṇa are identified with *haṁsas* (*Ṛgveda,* 9.97.8). But as a symbol *haṁsa* sometimes signified Indra (*Ṛgveda,* 10.124.9); but more often in the *Ṛgveda* and the *Atharvaveda* it referred to the Sun. But in the *Mādhyamdina-saṁhitā haṁsas,* ideal of the Ṛgvedic seers for their sweet voice, are recommended to be sacrificed for God Soma (*somāya haṁsān ālabhate,* 24.22)[1].

Haṁsa in the Older Upaniṣads

In the *Chāndogya Upaniṣad* (iv.i)[2] it was the conversation between two swans which gave an idea to *Jānaśruti* about Raikva, the Brahman-knower. Similarly when Satyakāma was accepted as a disciple by Hāridrumata Gautama, and sent to the forest to tend cattle, then on his way home it was a swan, who flew down and instructed him about a quarter of Brahman (*Chāndogya Upaniṣad* iv.7). Here the swan is represented as a teacher of Brahman. In the *Bṛhad-Āraṛyaka-Upniṣad* (4.3.11-12) Brahman is represented as a golden swan (*hiraṇmayaḥ puruṣa ekahaṁsaḥ*) which has resorted to this nest of the body (*avaraṁ kulāyam*) like a bird.

Haṁsa in the Old Upaniṣads

Besides the designation of the body as a nest the *Śvetāśvatara Upaniṣad* (*iii.*18) describes the human body as a dwelling with nine doors. And the *haṁsa* is said to be residing there. Brahman, the controller of the whole universe becomes embodied (*dehī*) in the nine-gated residence[3] (*navadvāre pure dehī haṁso lilāyate* bahis). Elsewhere (*Śvetāśvatara Upaniṣad* i.6) it is said, because of its being embodied and because of its regarding itself and the mover as different (*pṛthag ātmānam preritāram ca matvā)* the swan flutters about again and again in the *brahma-cakra*[4]. So there is only one *haṁsa* (the Supreme Self) that is imprisoned in this city of the human body, that rotates again and again in the *brahma-cakra,* and that has entered into this universe of name and form like the Sun setting in the sea.[5] Thus in the old *Upaniṣads* the Supreme Self is generally designated as the *haṁsa*, whereas the individual self is meant, when there is reference to its imprisonment in the nine-gated city of the body (*navadvārapura*) or in the common ordinary nest (*avara kulāya*).

Importance of 'Om'

The knowledge of Brahman, that is, *para vidyā* alone, can give a man immortality. But the Upaniṣadic seers had defined Brahman in a negative way as *neti neti* (*athāta ādeśo neti neti, Bṛhad-Āraṇyaka-Upaniṣad, 2.3.6*). It was very difficult to meditate upon the impersonal attributeless Brahaman. So in these old *Upaniṣads* 'Om' came to be used as the most important symbol of power that creates, sustains and destroys the world. It was regarded as the supreme *mantra* to be used in meditation.

'Om' pictured as haṁsa in the new Upaniṣads

Hinduism has always sought its inspiration in the Vedic Upaniṣads. Hence there has been ceaseless effort to compose new *Upaniṣads,* down to the sixteenth century at least. When these new Upaniṣads were composed, many new different interpretations came to be given of this '*Om*'. And the epithet *haṁsa* came to be substituted for '*Om*'. The *Dhyānabindu Upaniṣad*

(Verse No. 24)[6] speaks of this *Omkāra* as the *hamsa* stationed in the heart of all persons. And the *Parambrahma Upaniṣad* (p. 457) emphasises the *praṇava hamsa* to be symbolic of the Supreme Self (*praṇava hamsaḥ parambrahma*). In the *Nādabindu Upaniṣad* (Verse 1-5)[7] we get the complete picture of 'Om' as a *hamsa*. '*A*' is the right wing of the Supreme Self described as *hamsa;* '*U*' is the left wing; '*M*' is the tail. The *arddha-mātrā* is the head. Legs are the *guṇas Sattva, Rajas* and *Tamas*. Its body is said to be the truth. *Dharma* is the right eye; *adharma* is the left eye. *Bhūrloka* is its feet; its knees are *Bhuvarloka;* in its hip region is *Suvarloka*; in its navel region is *Maharloka*. The *Janaloka* is the region of its heart. *Tapoloka* is its throat. *Satyaloka* is established in the middle of its brows and forehead. Thus the *Omkāra* symbolising Brahman represented the entire universe and was pictured as a swan. By meditating on *praṇava-hamsa* (*Omkāra pictured as a swan*) one can rouse the *kuṇḍalinī*[8] and can enjoy the bliss of the Supreme Self.

Ajapā hamsamantra

The other way pointed out by the new *Upaniṣad* is the meditation of *hamsa-mantra*. At the time of inhaling and exhaling, the sounds '*ham*' and '*sa*' are produced; and thus without the actual muttering of it the *hamsa-mantra* is recited. Therefore, this is called *ajapā-hamsa-mantra (Yoga-cūḍāmaṇi Upaniṣad,* Verse 33). The same *Yoga-cūḍāmaṇi Upaniṣad* (verse 32)[9] says that the individual self goes out with the letter '*ha*' and enters again with the letter '*sa*'. The individual self is always uttering this *mantra* as '*hamsa*', '*hamsa*'.

The uttering of this *ajapā-hamsa-mantra* as completed at the six *cakras*[10] that is the six centres of subtle forces, within the course of one day and night is 21,606 times (*Hamsa Upaniṣad*, p. 132).[11] By meditating on this *hamsa-mantra* the Yogin attains ecstatic state of mind. If the seeker finds if difficult to meditate upon the *hamsātman* either of *saguṇa* form or of the *nirguṇa* kind, then he should have recourse silently to the prayer of this *ajapā-haṁsa-mantra,* through expiration and inspiration for days and nights together; and by such crores of prayers of this kind alone, he further experiences the *nāda-brahman* in the *anāhata cakra* (*Haṁsa Upaniṣad,* p. 132). The authors of the new *Upaniṣads* interpret the sound *haṁsa* in a very ingenious way. In *haṁsa* the sound *'ham'* is produced at the time of exhaling and '*sa*' is produced at the time of inhaling. When it is repeated, *haṁsa* becomes *so'ham.* In *Nārada-parivrājaka-Upaniṣad* (*Ṣaṣṭha Upadeśa,* p. 275)[12] the idea is put forth very clearly when it is said that *haṁsa* (the individual self) under the guise of inhaling and exhaling is muttering the *mantra so'ham,* and is trying to find out the reality. The *Brahmavidyā Upaniṣad* (verse 79)[13] speaks of this *haṁsa* in form of inhaling and exhaling as taking the form of *so'ham.* The interpretation of *haṁsa* in the *Yoga- cūḍāmaṇi Upaniṣad* (verses 82-83)[14] appears to be a little more ingenious. The 'sa' indicates *tvam-padārtha,* the individual self; the '*ha'* refers to *tat-padārtha,* the Supreme Self. When the 'sa' the individual self meditates "so'ham"–I am the Supreme Self, it becomes '*ha*'–the Supreme Self. The meditation on *oṃkāra* pictured as *haṁsa,* meditation of the *ajapāhaṁsamantra,* rousing of the *kuṇḍalinī* after taking recourse to breath-control–all these are the means for the realisation of the Supreme Self designated as *haṁsa.* And all these means are called *haṁsa-yoga* in the new *Upaniṣads. Haṁsavidyā* and *haṁsa-yoga* refer to one and the same discipline. The *Nādabindu Upaniṣad* (verses 5-6)[15] asserts that the person well-versed in this *haṁsa-yoga* is not at all affected by the hundreds of myriads of sins due to his past *karman.* The *Bhahma-vidyā Upaniṣad* (verse 26) likewise says that there is no other road to immortality than this *haṁsa-vidyā (haṁsavidyāmṛte loke nāsti nityatvasādhanam).* And the *Yogacūḍāmaṇi Upaniṣad* (verse 34)[16] goes a step further, and declares that there has never been, never shall be the like of this *vidyā,* the like of this *japa*, the like of this knowledge. The *haṁsa-vidyā* is spoken of as the great lore, as sacred and superb (*mahāvidyā, pāvanī* and *parā-Brahmavidyā Upaniṣad* Verse 26).

Tantric analysis of the haṁsa-mantra

The influence of *tantras* is clearly seen in the new *Upaniṣads*. When many sectarian gods and goddesses came to be worshipped, the new *Upaniṣads* recommended mystical *tantrik mantras* for their worship. For every *mantra* there was to be a seer, a metre, *śakti* (a mystical power presiding over the *mantra*), *kīlaka* (the protecting rod), purpose or motive of uttering the *mantra,* etc. When a *mantra* is uttered after mentioning all these details, then only it becomes fruitful, not otherwise. So the *ajapā-haṁsa-mantra* resting on the incoming and outgoing breath is also analysed from the *tantric* point of view. *Haṁsa* (the individual self) is the seer of this *mantra; paramahaṁsa* (the Supreme Self) is the deity; the metre is *avykta gāyatrī;* the seed (*bīja*) is *ham; śakti* is represented by the syllable 'saḥ'. The *kīlaka* is "so'ham". The *mantra* is uttered for obtaining the direct vision of the *haṁsātman (Haṁsa Upaniṣad,* p. 132).

Besides the *haṁsa mantra* even the four *mahāvākyas 'prajñānam brahma', 'aham brahmā smi', ayam ātmā brahma'* and *tat tvam asi'* have been analysed from the tantric point of view (*Śukarahasya Upaniṣad*, Chapter II, page 220). In the case of these so-called Vedantic *mantras*, *haṁsa* (the individual self) is the seer; and *paramahaṁsa* (the Supreme Self) is the deity (*Śukarahasya Upaniṣad,* Chapter II, page 220).

Composition of Haṁsa Gāyatrī

The famous *Gāyatrī mantra* in the *Ṛgveda* is stated with reference to *Savitṛ.*[17] The *Gāyatrī rahasya* and the *Gāyatrī Upaniṣads have discussed this gāyatrī mantra* syllable by syllable as the means of meditation and concentration. This *mantra* became so popular that all the later sects had *gāyatrī* composed with reference to their favourite deity. The composition of new *gāyatrī mantras* was taken up not only in the worship of the five principal deities (*pancāyatana pūjā Śiva, Viṣṇu, Devī, Sūrya* and *Gaṇapati*), but also it spreads to minor deities, nay even to abstract things like *jvara* and *kāma* etc. The *haṁsa* was also deified, and in order to suit this new deity a new *gāyatrī mantra* with only a few changes was necessary.

हंसहंसाय विद्महे सोऽहं हंसाय धीमहि
तन्नो हंसः प्रचोदयात्। *(Vanadurgā Upaniṣad)*[18]

This haṁsa-*gāyatrī* does not give the name of the deity-*haṁsa* in the first foot as in the original *gāyatrī mantra* (*tat Savituḥ*), but in the third, that is last foot, perhaps to bring out the greatness of the deity concerned. The imitation of the original *Ṛgvedic gāyatrī mantra* is the main feature of this *haṁsa-gāyatrī*.

Two Types of Saṁnyāsins, Haṁsa and Paramahaṁsa

The term *haṁsa* was used without any restriction for signifying the individual self as well as the Supreme Self. But side by side we see that the term *haṁsa* came to denote the individual self; and epithent '*paro*' was added to signify the Supreme Self. In the *Śvetāśvatara Upaniṣad* (4.6) and the *Muṇḍaka Upaniṣad* (3.1.1) the individual self and the Supreme Self have been represented as two birds (*dvā suparṇā*) sitting on the same tree. Following this the new *Upaniṣad Mantrikā* (verse 8) speaks of the individual self as *suparṇa pippalāśana (*the bird eating the sweet fruit) and of the supreme self as *udāsīna dhruva haṁsa (*the bird, eternal and indifferent*)*. In the *haṁsa Upaniṣad* (p. 132) the individual self is described as seated in the eight-petalled lotus of the heart (*aṣṭadale haṁsātman);* and the Supreme Self (*parama haṁsa*) is described as resembling a crore of suns (*bhānukoṭipratīkāśa*). On the basis of this division of the self as *haṁsa* and *paramahaṁsa, in some Upaniṣads* like *Bhikṣuka, Parama-hṁsa-parivrājaka* and *Śātyāyanīya* there are described four kinds of *Saṁnyāsins* in the ascending order[19]-*kutīcaka, bahūdaka, haṁsa* and *paramahaṁsa*. They clearly bring out the distinction between *haṁsa* and *paramahaṁsa*.

Characteristics of the Haṁsa Saṁnyāsin

The *haṁsa saṁnyāsin* takes bath only once a day. He should have only a fragment of the bath towel. He is distinguished by his matted hair. He does not shave his head. He is not to keep with him the least belongings. He should take that much of food which is begged as alms, and which can be contained in the palm of his hand. He is said to maintain on the urine of the cow, the cow-dung; and he observes the *cāndrāyaṇa* vow. His sect mark is *ūrdhvapuṇḍra* or a *tripuṇḍra*. *Hamṣa* does not worship gods. He does not utter any *mantra*. The *āntaḥpraṇava* and meditation on the Vedas are recommended for him. He does not stay at one place. He is supposed to stay for one night in a village, five nights in a city and seven nights in a holy place. He should be stationary for the four months of the rainy season.

Characteristics of the Paramahaṁsa Saṁnyāsin

Paramahaṁsa takes mental bath only; the abandonment of all the mental inclinations is the real bath for him. He is without any dress on his body. He is devoid of the tuft of hair; still he does not have a clean shave. He may possess a *Kaupīna* (loin-cloth) and one bamboo staff. The *paramahaṁsa* may or may not put on clothes. He should beg alms from five houses with his hands as the pot. He eats only eight morsels of food. He may beg alms from the house of a person belonging to any caste. Besmearing the body with the sacred ashes is the sect-mark for him. He is to practise mental worship only. The *āntaḥpraṇava* and meditation are prescribed for him. The *paramahaṁsa* in his outward appearance looks like a mad man. His characteristics are non-manifest. The *paramahaṁsa* has no belongings like the staff, the water-pot etc. He does not wear a religious thread. He is lustrous in his form. He has balanced mind; and he is well-versed in the knowledge of Brahman. He stays in a vacant house, temple, pastures, anthill, at the foot of a river, in the cave of a mountain or in the hollow of a tree. There are no rules or limitations of any sort for the *paramahaṁsa*. The *paramahaṁsa* is also said to possess the mark of *Viṣṇu*. He may preach the *mahāvākyas* like *tat tvam asi,* etc. Whereas the *haṁsa-saṁnyāsin* goes to *tapoloka,* the *paramahaṁsa* goes to *satyaloka.* Though the *paramahaṁsa-parivrājaka Upaniṣad* (p. 420) speaks of the number of the *paramahaṁsas* to be very limited, the *Jābāla Upaniṣad* (6th khaṇḍa) gives a list of some prominent ascetics of this order like *Saṁvartaka, Āruṇi, Śvetaketu, Durvāsas, Ṛbhu, Nidāgha, Jaḍabharata, Dattātreya* and *Raivataka.*

Both the kinds of Saṁnyāsins mentioned above are described as being on the path of *yoga,* and as desiring nothing but salvation. The difference between them is specially a difference of diet and other external things.

In the *Ṛgveda* the word *haṁsa* besides denoting the swan was also used as a symbol of the Sun. In the old Upaniṣads we find how the word came to mean both the individual self and the Supreme Self. In the post-Vedic period, when Purāṇic Hinduism was gaining strength, *haṁsa* became a popular symbol, and signified the different techniques of *yoga* and meditation. It is the new Upaniṣads which throw a flood of light on the concept of *haṁsa* and its development. R.R. Diwakar[20] rightly says–"In these *Upaniṣads* we have quite a few new strains of thought especially in the field of *yoga,* of ethics and tantrik worship. It is in these *Upaniṣads* that we came across a new pantheon and details of new spiritual practices."

References

* Prof. J. Ph. Vogel in his paper *'The goose (Sanskrit haṁsa) in Indian literature and art'*, Art and Letters, New Series, Vol. XXVII, 1953, pp. 17-24 suggests that the Sanskrit word *haṁsa* designates the goose.

1. सोमाय हंसान् आलभते वायवे बंलाका
   इन्द्राग्निभ्यां क्रुञ्चान् मित्राय मद्गून् वरुणाय चक्रवाकान्।।
2. Unless otherwise stated, all the Upaniṣadic texts referred to are from "One hundred and eight Upaniṣads" edited by V.L. Sh. Panśīkar, Bombay, 1932.
3. The *Kaṭhopaniṣad* (5.1) on the other hand speaks of the body as the elevan-gated citatel-the gates being two eyes, two ears, two nostrils, mouth, the two lower orifices, the navel and the *vidṛti.* By the omission of the last two the body is conceived of as a nine-gated city.
4. The same śloka is repeated in *Nāradaparibrājaka Upaniṣad* 9.5.
5. एको हंसो भुवनस्यास्य मध्ये
   स एवाग्नि: सलिले संनिविष्ट: (Śvetāśvatara Upaniṣad, 6.15)
6. गमागमस्थं गमनादिशून्यमोङ्कारमेकं रविकोटिदीप्तिम्।
   पश्यन्ति ये सर्वजनान्तरस्थं हंसात्मकं ते विरजा भवन्ति।।

7. अकारो दक्षिणः पक्ष उकारस्तूत्तरः स्मृतः।
मकारं पुच्छमित्याहुरर्धमात्रा तु मस्तकम्॥1॥
पादादिकं गुणास्तस्य शरीरं तत्वमुच्यते।
धर्माऽस्य दक्षिणं चक्षुः अधर्मोऽथ परः स्मृतः॥2॥
भूर्लोकः पादयोस्तस्य भुवर्लोकस्तु जानुनि।
सुवर्लोकः कटीदेशे नाभिदेशे महर्जगत्॥3॥
जनो लोकस्तु हृद्देशे कण्ठे लोकस्तपस्ततः।
भ्रुवोर्ललाटमध्ये तु सत्यलोको व्यवस्थितः॥4॥

8. The *Kuṇḍalinī* is a tangible and living symbol of the divine force, which when roused passes though *suṣumnā,* the principal *nāḍī* of the human being.

9. हकारेण वर्हियाति सकारेण विशेत् पुनः।
हंस हंसेत्यमुं मन्त्रं जीवो जपति सर्वदा॥

10. *Cakras* like *Mūlādhāra, Svādhiṣṭhana, Maṇipura, Anāhata, Viśuddhi* and *Ājñā* are the centres of the subtle forces. Their position is on the spinal cord.

11. The *Brahmavidyā Upanīṣad* (Verse 79) speaks of this number as 21,600. The *Amṛtanāda Upaniṣad* (Verse 34) speaks of the number of breaths as 1,13,180 (One lakh, thirteen thousand and one hundred eighty). When this number is shared by *Prāṇa, Apāna, Samāna, Udāna* and *Vyāna* the five vital airs, the share for each comes to exact 22,636 in 24 hours. On the other hand Mādhavācārya while speaking of this *ajapā-mantra* in *Pātañjala-Yoga-Darśana* speaks of 21,600 inspirations and expirations produced in course of a day and a night (*Sarvadarśana, saṁgraha,* Ānandāśrama Sanskrit Series, 1950, p. 138). The commentator Upaniṣad-*Brahmayogin* attributes this difference in number of breathing to difference of age and condition of the body.

12. जीवत्वं घटाकाशमहाकाशवद् व्यवधाने अस्ति। व्यवधानवशाद् एव हंसः सोऽहम् इति मन्त्रेण उच्छ्वासनिःश्वासव्यपदेशेन अनुसन्धानं करोति। एवं विज्ञाय शरोराभिमानं त्यजेत्।

13. सहस्रमेकं ह्ययुतं षट्शतं चैव सर्वदा।
उच्चरन् पठितो हंसः सोऽहम् इति अभिधीयते॥

14. सकारः खेचरी प्रोक्तस्त्वं पदं चेति निश्चितम्।
हकारः परमेशः स्यात् तत्पदं च इति निश्चितम्।
सकारो ध्यायते जन्तुर्हकारो हि भवेद् ध्रुवम्॥

15. एवमेतां समारूढो हसंयोगविचक्षणः।
न भिद्यते कर्मचारैः पापकोटिशतैरपि॥

16. अनया सदृशी विद्या अनया सदृशो जपः।
अनया सदृशं ज्ञानं न भूतं न भविष्यति।।

17. The muttering of this *gāyatrī mantra* forms the main topic in the morning, mid-day and evening adorations of the Brahmins. The text of the *mantra* is :

ओं भूर्भुवः स्वः तत् सवितुर्वरेण्यं भर्गो देवस्य धीमहि।
धियो यो नः प्रचोदयात्।

18. *Unpublished Upaniṣad.* The Adyar Library, Madras, 1933, p 463.

19. *The Saṁnyāsa Upaniṣad* (2.13) speaks of six types of saṁnyāsins in the ascending order : *Kuticaka, bahūdaka, haṁsa, paramahaṁsa, turīyātīta* and *avadhūta.*

20. Foreword to Neo-Upaniṣadic Philosophy by K.V. *Gajendragadkar,* Bhāratīya Vidyā Bhavan, 1959.

CHAPTER 6

Concept of Smaraṇa : Its Origin and Development

The *Bhagavadgītā* is the basic text of Vaiṣṇavite theology. Many ideas found in this text have been developed later in texts like Purāṇas and Smṛtis. The *Viśva-rūpa-darśana*[1] where Śrīkṛṣṇa shows the whole universe to be within him is found repeated in many different contexts in the Purāṇa-literature[2]. Another concept which became very popular in later Hinduism is remembrance (*smaraṇa*) at the death-bed referred to in *Gītā* (Chapter-VIII.5) In this verse Śrīkṛṣṇa says to Arjuna–"The man who remembering me alone in his last moments departs from this life, comes to me, there is no doubt about it." From this one may naturally infer that inspite of a sinful and vicious life led by a man in his past life, the thoughts of the man at the approach of death decide his future. But the author of the *Gītā* emphasises that a man's spirit is engrossed by the thoughts that he has entertained throughout his life; a man can think of spiritual matters or about God at the time of death, only if he has been thinking about such matters or about God throughout his life. The *Gītā* (Chapter-VIII.6) continues : "whichever form or thing a man remembers when he leaves the body at death, to that alone he goes, having been always (through out his life) engrossed in meditating over it."

We can trace the germs of this idea in the Upaniṣadic literature. In the *Chāndogya Upaniṣad* (III.14.1) the worshipper is directed to meditate on the highest Brahman. "All this is Brahman. A man should meditate on that from which the universe originates, in which it is dissolved, and by which it is sustained. Now a man is the creature of his will (*Kratumayah puruṣa*).[3]

According to whatever is his will or thought in this world, so will he become after departing from this world." *The Praśna Upaniṣad* (III. 10) contains a similar idea. It is here asserted that it is the thought-power or the will that raises the soul higher and higher. Together with whatever thought he had at the time of death, he enters into *Prāna* (*yaccitah tena eṣa prānam āyāti....* yathāsamkalpitam lokam nayati). *Prāṇa,* in combination with *Udāna*, and in association with the soul, leads him to the world desired by him. Thus the concept of remembrance at the time of death though presented in very clear terms in the *Gītā* (Chapter-VIII, 5.6) has its germs already in the Upaniṣads.

In course of time it came to be a strong belief with the Hindus that the thoughts a dying man entertains at the time of death, determine what will happen to his spirit after physical death; therefore, when death approaches, a man should give up all thoughts of mundane affairs and all earthly attachments, should think of his favourite deity, should inaudibly recite *Om namo Vāsudevāya*–the eight syllabled *mantra* in honour of Viṣṇu. When the dying man is on the verge of collapse, and is unable to recite holy names of his favourite deity, it was recommended by several texts that the dying man should be made to listen to holy Vedic texts[4]. The *Gautamapitṛmedha–sūtra* (I.1-8) prescribes that when one's father, mother, brother, teacher or any of his brahmin friends is on his death bed, one should make the dying man hear the first and the last verses of the Veda and certain *sāmans,* and should utter in the dying man's right ear one *sāman,* The *Ṛgvidhāna*[5] provides that one should repeat at the time of death the *sūkta* beginning with *nānānam*, that is *Ṛgveda* IX–112. The *Hiraṇya-keśi-pitṛmedhasūtra* (I.1) provides that when it is thought that the *āhitāgni* is going to die, the son or some near relative should mutter in the dying man's ear (if he is a knower of Brahman) the two *anuvākas of the Taittirīya Upaniṣad* (II.1 and III.1) beginning with *brahmavid āpnoti param* and *bhṛgur vai vāruṇih.* The Antyakarmadīpaka[6] says that if a dying man is unable to engage in *japa,* he should resolve in his mind the benign form of Viṣṇu or Śiva, the *Bhagavadgītā,* the *Bhāgavata,* the *Mahābhārata,* the *Rāmāyaṇa,* the *Upaniṣads* like *Īśāvāsya* and hymns to Soma. The preceding account helps us in tracing the development of the concept of *smaraṇa* propounded in the famous *Gītā śloka* (VIII.5).

Now we turn our attention to the Purāṇa literature, where this idea of *smaraṇa* is treated in greater details, The *Viṣṇupurāṇa*[7] (II.13) narrates the interesting story of the king Bharata. Leaving his kingdom, his children and all his friends, the king used to live in Śālagrāma *tīrtha.* Once he had gone to a river for bath, there he found a newly born deer after whose delivery the female mother-deer died. The king took the fawn to his hermitage, where he tended it, and fed it every day. Long absence of the deer from the hermitage used to worry him; and the king was animated with great pleasure at the sight of the fawn. The king died, watched by the deer with tears in its eyes like a son mourning for his father. The king himself, as he expired, cast his longing eyes upon the animal, and thought of nothing else, being wholly occupied with one idea. In consequence of this predominant feeling at such a time, the king was born again in Jambumārga forest as a deer with the faculty of remembering his former life[8]. Stories of this type always preach the importance of *smaraṇa,* specially at the approach of death.

With the development of Vaiṣṇavism evolved a new form of Viṣṇu–worship founded on the doctrine of *bhakti.* The concept of *bhakti* though traced to *Ṛgvedic* hymns addressed to Indra or Varuṇa and to some passages of the *Śvetāśvatara-Upaniṣad*, finds its first clear exposition in the *Gītā*. Gradually with the spread and development of Vaiṣṇavism *bhakti* becomes the only means of liberation. In *Viṣṇupurāṇa* (I.17-20) is narrated the story of the great devotee Prahlāda, who is saved from all the calamities because of his devotion to Viṣṇu. As we shall presently see, the devotion or *bhakti* of Prahlāda in *Viṣṇupurāṇa* consists only of *smaraṇa.* In the second meeting of Prahlāda with his father Hiraṇyakaśipu, the latter persuades his son to give up glorifying Viṣṇu. But Prahlāda is reluctant, and tells his father that he cannot give up his devotion to Viṣṇu, because "the recollection of Viṣṇu (*yasmin smṛte*) alone is sufficient to dissipate all the perils consequent upon birth, old age or death".[9] Then Hiraṇya-kaśipu commands the serpents to bite his son to death, but Prahlāda feels no pain from their bites, because "he is immersed in rapturous recollections of Viṣṇu" (*tatsmṛty āhlāda–susthitah,* I.17.39). The next ordeal put before Prahlāda was that he was assailed by the elephants of the quarters; but this plan of Hiraṇykaśipu did not succeed; rather the tusks of elephants became blunt because Prahlāda thought of Govinda.[10] Then Prahlāda asserts before his father that remembrance of Janārdana is his defence against any great fearful calamity.[11] Afterwards Prahlāda is put in fire, there also he remains unhurt. Then on the advice of his priests Hiraṇyakaśipu sends back his son to the school. There in the school in leisure hours Prahlāda advises his classmates to remember Viṣṇu, because that is the means for being liberated from this bondage of the earth (*Viṣṇuḥ smaryatām* bandhamuktidaḥ, I.17.77). The reason Prahlāda cites for remembering Viṣṇu is that *smaraṇa* is so easy a job and the rewards of *smaraṇa* are so rich.[12] When Hiraṇyakaśipu is reported about this, he advises the cooks to give deadly poison in his food. Prahlāda takes that food after having sanctified it by uttering the name of Viṣṇu (anantoccāraṇena..... *abhimantrya*, I.18.5), so no injury comes to him. Once again when the demon-chief hurled him down from the top of his palace, the mother Earth received him gently on her lap, because Prahlāda was remembering Hari in his heart (*hṛdayena udvahan Harim,* I.19.12). Then Śambara, the mightiest of enchanters employs magic device to kill Prahlāda, but when the boy in a tranquil heart directed his thoughts to the destroyer of Madhu (*sasmāra Madhusudanam* I.19.18), Viṣṇu sent his discus Sudarśana to defend the youth. The boy is put to further ordeals. His angry father commands the cold withering wind to penetrate into the body of Prahlāda, but Viṣṇu seated in his heart drinks up the fearful wind, because the boy very intently and devotedly thinks of Viṣṇu (*hṛdayena mahātmānam dadhāra dharanī-dharam,* I, 19.23). Thus for Prahlāda *smaraṇa* is the only effective weapon in all types of dangers and difficulties. Besides the terminologies like *smṛti, smaraṇa, anusmaraṇa* the

Viṣṇupurāṇa uses other related expressions like *uccāraṇa, hṛdayena udvahan, hṛdayena dadhāra.*

Prahlāda's *smaraṇa* of Viṣṇu is out of devotion and regard. But the same *Viṣṇupurāṇa* teaches another type of *smaraṇa-smaraṇa* through hatred. In this Purāṇa (IV.15.17) it is said that Śiśupāla was first born as Hiraṇyakaśipu. In this life though he was killed by Viṣṇu, he did not recognise him to be so; because the divinity at that time had assumed the body of a man and a lion. But even though he did not get liberation because he was killed at the hands of Viṣṇu, with unlimited power and enjoyment he was born as Rāvana, the sovereign of the three worlds. Again Rāvaṇa though killed by Rāma could not know that the son of Daśaratha was really Viṣṇu, because his mind was engrossed completely by the thoughts of Jānaki. But just because of his being killed by Viṣṇu Rāvaṇa was reborn as Śiśupāla in the illustrious family of the kings of Cedi with an extensive dominion. In this life as the king of Cedis, in many connections the names of Viṣṇu were brought to his notice; and on all these occasions the enmity that had accumulated through successive births influenced his mind. Always with disrespect Śiśupāla used to utter the different names of Viṣṇu. At the time of being killed by Sudarśana discus he was uttering the names of Viṣṇu in malediction; he was thinking of the Lord in his heart out of enmity; he could recognise his killer to be Viṣṇu. So all his sins were washed off because of remembering Him, and he was merged in Viṣṇu (*Viṣṇupurāṇa,* IV.15.15).

It is taught here that Viṣṇu is the essence of liberation. To be killed by Him is always blissful. If at the time of being killed by Viṣṇu, one hatefully remembers Him and recognises the divinity to be Viṣṇu, then one gets liberation. But even if one does not remember Him, and one does not recognise Him to be Viṣṇu, still just because of being killed by Him one gets a better reward, a new life in a higher position like Rāvaṇa or Śiśupāla.

The *Viṣṇupurāṇa* represents an earlier phase in the development of Vaiṣṇavism. But when we come to *Bhāgavata* we find that here the concept of *bhakti* has changed. When asked by Hiranyakaśipu about the lesson he has learnt from his teacher, Prahlāda speaks of nine features of *bhakti*[13] like listening to the holy names of Viṣṇu, reciting them, recollection of them, doing service at His lotus-feet, worshipping Him, adoring Him, serving Him, self-abnegation for the sake of meditation upon Him. For Prahlāda of *Viṣṇupurāṇa bhakti* consists only of *smaraṇa.* But for Pralāda of *Bhāgavata bhakti* is nine-fold and *smaraṇa* is one of these nine-features. In *Bhāgavata* (VII.9.14) Prahlāda recommends the recollection of the terrible man-lion form for being fearless,-O Man-lion, people remember your (terrible) form to get rid of fear (*sarve rūpam nṛsimha vibhayāya janāḥ-smaranti*). The *Viṣṇupurāṇa* speaks of *smaraṇa* through hatred (*ākrośa*) as is the case with Śiśupāla. The *Bhāgavata* (VII. 1.27-28) adds to it another motive–that is *smaraṇa* through fear. The idea is presented through a nice simile. The black bee brings the cockroach inside its hole; the insect cockroach through fear and anxiety (*saṁrambha-bhaya-yogena*) thinks intently of the black bee, and attains its form. So also when through fear and anxiety one constantly thinks of the Lord as one's bitter enemy, one can attain Him. The *Brahmapurāṇa*[14] (Chapter-216.88) goes one step further, and declares that " those men who always remember Janārdana even by roguery (śāṭhyena), go to the world of Viṣṇu after death. Commenting upon this inveterate habit of exaggeration of the authors of the Purāṇas, Kane[15] says, "The author or authors of Purāṇas often wrote like modern advertisers of medicines, toilet articles etc."

Now we take up the question of *smaraṇa,* in other spheres of religion. As in Buddhism, Islam and Christianity so also pilgrimage to holy *tirthas* was recommended in Hinduism. The *Viṣṇu-Dharma-Sūtra* (II.16.17) among other characteristics of *Dharma* like *satya, dayā, kṣamā,* speaks of visit to holy places (tīrthānusaraṇa) as one of the features of *dharma.* In the *Viṣṇudharmottara Purāṇa*[16] visit of holy places is spoken of as one of the *sāmānya-dharmas.* Once the holy places attained prominence, not only visit to those places was recommended, but *smaraṇa* of those places also was said to be blissful. The *Matsyapurāṇa*[17] lays down that "in his own country or house or after leaving his country, if a man dies on the way to Prayāga, he gets the world of *Brahma* without reaching Prayāga provided he dies remembering it" Like Prayāga the Ganges had, and still has a great spiritual influence on the Hindu mind. Because very highly esteemed *tīrthas* are situated on its banks, there is a grand eulogy of the Ganges in the Epics and the Purāṇas. According to *Mahābhārata,*[18] the Ganges if its name is uttered, purifies a sinner (*punāti kīrtiatā pāpam*).

References

1. In Chapter XI of the *Bhagavadgītā* Śrīkṛṣṇa shows his Universal Form to Arjuna "who understands the meaning of the cosmic process and destiny."
2. In *Matsyapurāṇa* (Anandasrama Edition, Chapt. 246. 52-70) Vali after he has offered the water for making a gift, sees the whole universe existing in the dwarf form of Viṣṇu. In *Viṣṇupurāṇa* (Gita Press Edition, 5.1.34-50) when Brahmā goes along with the gods to the resting place of Viṣṇu, the northern shore of the milky ocean, and recites a long hymn of praise, Viṣṇu shows his Universal Form. In *Padma Purāṇa* (Anandasrama Edition, 5.42. 87–96), when the man-lion appears in the assembly of Hiraṇyakaśipu, Prahlāda sees the whole universe in his body.
3. The term *'kratu'* literally means in Vedic literature plan, intention; resolution, determination, purpose and understanding. It is translated here as 'will' or thought'.
4. In Orissa *Bhāgavatapurāṇa* is recited near a man at the death-bed. In Northern India because of the popularity of the Rama cult the *Tulasi Rāmāyaṇa* is recited on the occasion. It is the usual custom with Hindus in Northern India that when the dead body is put on bamboo poles, and carried to the cremation ground, the mourner cry–"Rāma Rāma, the true name" (Rāma; Rāma, satya nāma). This name itself representing an incarnation of Viṣṇu, when pushed into the ears of dead man, has power to defeat the emissaries of Yama, and to secure certain admittance to the world of Viṣṇu.
5. *Ṛg-vidhāna.* 111. 19-20 Edited by J.L. Shastri, Lahore, 1940.
6. *Antyakarmadīpaka* of Nityananda Edited in Kashi Sanskrit Series. P. 18.

7. *Viṣṇupurāṇa,* Gītā Press Edition, Saṁvat 2024
8. *Viṣṇupurāṇa,* II. 13.32-33
 mṛgameva tadādrākṣīttyajanprāṇānasāvapi
 tanmayatvena maitreya nānyatkiṁcidacintayat
 tataśca tatkālakṛtāṁ bhāvanāṁ prāpya tādṛśīm
 jambumarge mahāraṇye jato jātismaro mṛgaḥ
9. *Viṣṇupurāṇa,* 1.17.36
 yasmin smṛte janmajar āntakādi
 bhayāni sarvāṇyapayānti tāta//
10. *Viṣṇupurāṇa,* 1.17.43
 smaratastasya Govindamibhadantāḥ
 sahasraśaḥ
 śīrṇā vakṣasthalaṁ prāpya
11. *Viṣṇupurāṇa,* 1.17.44
 mahāvipat-tāpavināśanoyam
 janārdanānusmaraṇānubhāvaḥ
12. *Viṣṇupurāṇa,* 1.17.78
 prayāsaḥ smaraṇe kosyasmṛto yacchati śobhanam
 pāpakṣayaśca bhavati smaratāṁ tam aharniśam//
13. *Bhāgavatapurāṇa,* Gītā Press Edition, VII, 5.23
 śravaṇaṁ kīrtanaṁ viṣṇoh smaraṇaṁ pādasevanam
 arcanaṁ vandanaṁ dāsyaṁ sakhyamātmanivedanam
14. *Brahmapurāṇa,* Anandāśrama Edition.
15. P.V. Kane–*History of Dharma-śāstra,* Vol. V, Part-I 1958, p. 254
16. *Viṣṇudharmottara-purāṇa,* Venkatesvara Press, Edition II, 80.1-4.
17. *Matsya-purāṇa,* Ānandāśrama Edition, 105, 8-9 :
 deśastho yadivāraṇye videśasthothav āgṛhe/
 prayāgaṁ smaramāṇopi yastuprāṇān parityajet/
 brahmalokamavāpnoti vadantī ṛṣipuṁgavāḥ//
18. *Mahābhārata,* Gītā Press Edition, Saṁvat 2013. Vanaparva, 85.93.

CHAPTER 7

The Concept of Alakṣmī

In the tenth Maṇḍala of the *ṚgVeda*, the term, 'Lakṣmī' appears in the context of sign or mark-*bhadrā eṣā lakṣmīḥ nihitādhivācī* (R.V. 10,71,2) "their speech retains the blessed sign imprinted". The epithet applied to *lakṣmī* in this context is *bhadrā'*. When we come to *Atharva Veda,* we notice Lakṣmī described from two aspects. She is Puṇyā and at the same time she is called Pāpī Lakṣmī. Like most of the *mantras* of the *Atharva Veda* used for driving off evil spirits by magical device, we find reference to different rites in the *Atharva Veda* for driving off this Pāpī-Lakṣmī. After the merger of the auspicious Lakṣmī with Śrī, the goddess of beauty, the path became clear for the development of the Pāpī Lakāmī as a separate and an independent deity.

In the *Atharva Veda* which records the customs and traditions of the common people, we came across certain verses as a testimony to this in a propitiatory rite against Pāpī Lakṣmī–

प्र पतेत: पापि लक्ष्मि श्येत: प्रामुत: पत।
अयस्मयेनांकेन द्विषते त्वा सजामसि।। (7.115-1)

Fly forth from here O evil sign (Pāpī Lakṣmī), disappear from here, fly forth from yonder; with a hook of metal (ayasmaya) we attach you to him that hates us (A.V. 7,115,1) This Pāpī Lakṣmī was taken to be terribly harmful deity to the society. She was thought to be a flying substance sticking to one's body like a creeper to a tree–

या मा लक्ष्मी: पतयालू–रजुष्टाभिचस्कन्द वन्दनेव वृक्षम्।
अन्यत्रास्मात् सवितस्तामितो धा हिरण्यहस्तो वसु नो रराण:।।
(7, 115, 2)

'The unenjoyable flying Lakṣmī that hath mounted me as a creeper to a tree-that O Savitar may you put hence elsewhere than us, being golden-handed, granting good to us.

In A.V. 1.18.1[1] That Lakṣmī which intended to be driven away and which is at the same time an 'arāti' is nothing but the same Pāpī Lakṣmī; she is conceived to be very harmful which frustrates good intentions and disturbs happiness. She is likewise conceived as a demoniac being—

रिश्यपदीं वृषदतीं गोषेधं विधमामुत।
विलीढ्यं ललाम्यं ता अस्मन्नाशयामसि।। (A.V. 1, 18, 4)

"Antelope-footed, bull-toothed, the kine-repelling, the outblowing, the licked-out, the pallid (A.V. 1, 18, 4)."

1. Nirṛti

These very *mantras* of the *Atharva Veda* (7, 115, 1-4) which are used to drive away Pāpī Lakṣmī are prescribed by the Kauśika Sūtra (18, 16-18) for driving off Nirṛti. In the Ṛgveda (10.95, 14) she is mentioned as a malignant deity of death and destruction. In the V.S. (39, 13) she is related along-with Antaka and Mṛtyu.

The Gṛhya Sūtras prescribe a number of rites for propitiation of this malignant deity Nirṛti. When the baby becomes one year old, the *Śāṅkhāyana Gṛhya Sūtra* (1, 26, 16–17) prescribes sacrifices for Nirṛti alongwith Indra and Jyeṣṭhā.

Like the two-sided development of Lakṣmī-Pāpī-Lakṣmī and Puṇyā Lakṣmi, the T.B. (1, 6, 1, 1) refers to Nirṛti and Anumati. Before the performance of Rājasūya sacrifice two cakes are prepared, one for Nirṛti and the other for Anumati. First of all the offering is made to Nirṛti with the formula-go away *svāhā* rejoicing in the oblations. This is your share, O Nirṛti, the mighty one, you are rich in oblations, free him from anxiety or distress *(aṁhas)*. Whereas Nirṛti frees the sacrificer from *aṁhas*, distress and narrowness, Anumati points away the way to the sky.

By the time of the Kauśika Sūtra this malignant deity Nirṛti had already been identified with Pāpī Lakṣmī. This is why the

Kauśika Sūtra in prescribing a Śāntikalpa "propitiatory rite" against Nirṛti enjoins the recitation of four *mantras* of the *Atharva Veda* (7, 115, 1-4) which actually speak of Pāpī Lakṣmī. Before the commencement of the *puṣṭika* ceremony, a Śāntikalpa propitiatory rite against Nirṛti is prescribed by the Kauśika Sūtra. The rite is prescribed thus : In order to get rid of Nirṛti's evil influence the sacrificer has to wear black cloth and start the function beside a pool or a lake. He has to offer the old and worn-out shoes and umbrellas in the fire. Then the sacrificer has to pierce an iron nail in the thigh of a black crow which is used as a scape-goat. The same black crow is identified with Nirṛti, the evil deity. Some cakes are tied to the nail in the thigh of a crow facing towards the Nairṛta (South West) direction and one has to recite the *mantra* (A.V. 7, 115,1). Then the crow is allowed to fly away together with it the black Nirṛti and was expected to stick to one's enemies. The sacrificer has to use the black clothes as the under garment, a red garment as the upper dress and a white cloth as a turban. First of all, he has to take out the white turban with a piece of iron and has to throw it into the water with the *mantra* prescribed in A.V. (7, 115, 2).

While uttering the hymn (A.V. 7, 115, 3) he has to throw away the red clothes by the help of a piece of iron–

एकशतं लक्ष्म्यो मर्त्यस्य साकं तन्वा जनुषोऽधि जाताः।
तासां पापिष्ठा निरितः प्र हिण्मः शिवा अस्मभ्यं जातवेदो नि यच्छ।।

'A hundred and one are the Lakṣmī of a mortal, born from his birth together with his body; the worst of these we send forth out from us, O Jātavedas, confirm propitious (*Śivā*) Lakṣmī. Lastly the sacrificer has to throw away the black clothes by the help of the piece of iron into the water. It was believed that this black Nirṛti was just like an entity sticking to a person like a creeper to a tree. So by this magical rite of throwing away the used-up shoes, umbrellas as well as the clothes worn by one, it was believed that the sacrificer would be immune from the evil influence of the malignant deity, Nirṛti. Thus after propitiating Nirṛti outside near some pool or lake, the sacrificer has to return home to start with the *Puṣṭika* ceremony. By this way the sacrificer has to free himself from the evil spirit Nirṛti.'

This Nirṛti., who is no other than Pāpī Lakṣmī, is also-found mentioned alongwith a deity Asamṛddhi, an abstract concept deified. For attaining good fortune one has to drive off this oppressive deity. This Nirṛti or Pāpī Lakṣmī for whose propitiation the sacrificer of the Vedic age was so keen, has developed later to be Alakṣmī, the goddess famous for creating misery and misfortune.

2. *Alakṣmī in the Ṛgveda*

In the *Ṛgveda* we come across the hymn 155 in the tenth Maṇḍala. In the verse No. 1 of the hymn, an evil spirit called Sadānvā is addressed thus–

अरायि काणे विकटे
गिरिं गच्छ सदान्वे।

'Go to the hill, O Sadānvā, one-eyed hideous, ever screaming, (famine) we frighten you away with those heroes (lit. beings) of the 'cloud'. In the third *mantra* the evil spirit with a wicked looking chin is requested to take recourse to that far-off wood in the sea, that has no connection with human-beings and go to distant lands with it.

अदः यद् दारु प्लवते सिन्धोः पारे अपुरुषम्।
तत् आरभस्व दुर्हणो तेन गच्छ परः तरम्।। (R.V. 10, 155, 3)

The Anukramaṇi designates this hymn as Alakṣmīghna sūkta. Yāska in his *Nirukta* (VI. 30) commenting upon the first *mantra* says that Śirimbiṭha is the name of the seer Bharadvāja. Endowed with black ears Bharadvāja destroyed Alakṣmī with this *mantra*–

शिरिम्बिठः भरद्वाजः कालकर्णोपोतः
अलक्ष्मी निर्नाशयां चकार।

Saunaka in his *Bṛhaddevatā* speaks of this hymn as destructive of Alakṣmī यदरायित्यलक्ष्मीघ्नं (8,60) Ṛg Vidhāna also speaks of this as Alakṣmīnāśana Sūkta (?). Later commentators following the tradition have traced the concept of Alakṣmī in the hymn (R.V. 10,155). Durgācārya (the commentator of *Nirukta*) who can be placed about the thirteenth century A.D., following the traditional interpretation in commenting on the first *mantra* of this so-called Alakṣmīghna Sūkta, gives Alakṣmī as one of the meanings of Sadānvā. The great commentator Sāyaṇācārya follows the Niruktakāra and among other meanings of Sadānvā-

सर्वदा आक्रोशकारिणी दुर्भिक्षादि देवता

(The presiding deity of famine, always ready to do mischief) also gives the meaning of Alakṣmī. In the third *mantra* of this hymn with reference to the log of wood floating in the ocean, although in his first interpretation he connects the wood with the image of Puruṣottama, yet in the second interpretation he brings in the concept of Alakṣmī and interprets the word.

दुर्हणो–दुःखेन हननीय (or)
दुष्ट हनुयुक्त अलक्ष्मी

Thus beginning from Yāska to Sāyaṇa all the commentators have tried to find the trace of Alakṣmī in the hymn (R.V.10,155). Because of the use of the expressions like–*Arāyi* (unholy), *Kāṇe* (one-eyed), *Vikaṭe* (hideous), commentators have been allured to connect all these epithets with Alakṣmī, but when the Lakṣmī concept itself is absent in the *ṚgVeda* proper, we cannot imagine the goddess Alakṣmī to be referred to anywhere. The hymn is really directed against some evil spirit called Sadānvā; the evil spirit is asked to resort to a boat or a log of wood as a scape-goat and to go to a far-off region where there are no human-beings. The witch Sadānvā can be said to represent one of those witches who cause disease and disaster. Like other witches and demons she is driven away to mountains or high lands which lie on the otherside of the ocean. Though she possesses some features of Alakṣmī, but she is not the same as the well-known Alakṣmī whom we meet so often in the Gṛhya Sūtras and the Purāṇas. But the clear reference to Alakṣmī is noticed not in the *ṚgVeda* itself but in the appended hymns (Khila Sūkta) which were composed between the period of the Brāhmaṇas and *Upaniṣads*.[2]

3. Alakṣmī in the Śrī-Sūkta

Śrī-Sūkta occurring in the appended hymns of the *ṚgVeda* is the earliest record of the goddess Śrī-Laksmī; in this appended hymn we find reference to goddess Alakṣmī. Scheftelowitz[3] who had made a thorough analysis of Śrī-Sūkta rightly designates the three verses (6-8) as related to Alakṣmī. The verse 8 of the hymn[4] says-O Alakṣmī, squalid with hunger and thirst, the elder sister (of fortune), I repel you. Take away from my dwelling all sorts of poverty and misery'. In the verse 6[5] of the hymn-the cryptogamous *bilva* tree is said to be generated by reason of the austerities of goddess Śrī. The seer terribly afraid of Alakṣmī prays for her blessings so that through her favour the fruits of the *bilva* tree may prevent Alakṣmī within and without.

The *Bṛhaddevatā* (v. 91-2) states that the whole of Śri-Sūkta which is benediction, can be utilised with profit for driving off Alakṣmī from house.

श्रीसूक्तं आशीर्वादस्तु तत् स्यात् वा अलक्ष्मी अपनुदम्।

4. Origin of Alakṣmī

In the Brāhmaṇas one can notice that the old gods of the *ṚgVeda* have faded. Some gods like Viṣṇu and Rudra or Śiva have attained far greater prominence in the Brāhmaṇas, but above all stands Prajāpati who is the paramount lord of all creatures. The author of the Brāhmaṇas in glorifying Prajāpati[6] ascribed to him the origin of both the gods and the demons. Likewise Śrī is depicted as coming out of the severe penance of Prajāpati (S.B. 2, 4, 3, 1) and Jyeṣṭhā-Lakṣmī originated from the barren place on the forehead of Prajāpati (T.B. 2, 1, 2, 2).

With the development of Vaiṣṇavism, Viṣṇu became the pre-eminent god. The function of creation ascribed to Prajāpati is found transferred to Viṣṇu. The *Liṅga-Purāṇa* (2, 6, 3-5) says that Viṣṇu created the universe in two-fold ways. One part consisted of Śrī-Padmā, four Vedas, the rites prescribed by the Vedas and the Brāhmaṇas. And the other part consisted of Alakṣmī, Adharma and the rites deprecated by the Vedas. The same text continues, Viṣṇu created Alakṣmī first and later he created Lakṣmī (*Liṅga* P. 2. 6, 5). The *Brahmavaivarta Purāṇa* (1, 8, 10) narrates the birth of Adharma, and Alakṣmī from the back and left side of the creator (Dhātā).

The diversity in the description of the origin of Alakṣmī is definitely due to the fact that the Purāṇas are the collection of texts of heterogenous nature. Prof. Kirfel[7] who has made thorough study on Purāṇa literature has given us the real original Purāṇa texts which have been copied and elaborated by the redactors of the later period. In those original texts under the chapter *Sarga* and *Pratisarga* there is found the description of the birth of Lakṣmī. In this description of the primary creation Dakṣa in union with Prasūti gives birth to twenty four daughters like-Śraddhā, Dhṛti, Tuṣṭi. etc. among which Lakṣmī is one.[8] Again in the original text-kernal under the same chapter *Sarga* and *pratisarga*-Lakṣmī is described as the daughter of Bhṛgu and Khyāti[9]. Thus in the Urtext the origin of Lakṣmī is depicted sometimes as the daughter of Dakṣa and Prasūti and sometimes as the daughter of Bhṛgu and Khyāti. But nowhere in the birth account of Lakṣmī there is any mention of Alakṣmī. So it can be very easily concluded that after Alakṣmī attained prominence, and after she was represented as having all the opposite characteristics of Lakṣmī, her origin came to be associated with her so-called sister Lakṣmī. Besides making Viṣṇu as the creator of both Lakṣmī and Alakṣmī the interesting legend of the churning of the ocean[10] was also utilised by the redactors of the Purāṇas to trace the account of Alakṣmī.

It is a well known fact that the myth of the churning of the ocean, though first traced to the *Rāmāyaṇa* (1, 44) has gradually been taken up by later redactors of the Purāṇas. The elaboration has gone to such an extent that whereas in the *Rāmāyaṇa* the number of entities churned out of the ocean were six, the number of entities has risen up to eighteen in the version of the *Skanda*

Purāṇa. In most of the Purāṇas Lakṣmī was the entity to come out of the ocean. Rather in some of the Purāṇas the churning of the ocean has solely been taken for getting Lakṣmī.[11] Gradually with the spread of Vaiṣṇavism the Purāṇas like *Viṣṇu Purāṇa* and *Bhāgavata Purāṇa* have depicted the rise of Lakṣmī from the ocean with more grandeur and imagination. Only when a very close relation developed between Lakṣmī and Alakṣmī, only when it was found that propitiation of Alakṣmī and blessings of Lakṣmī both are necessary for making one's life happy and cheerful, both the birth of Lakṣmī and Alakṣmī were put together in one account. Moreover, sisterly relation though not so cordial, developed between Lakṣmī and Alakṣmī. In consequence the Purāṇakāras depicting the birth of Lakṣmī from the churning of the ocean were enamoured to trace the birth of Alakṣmī from the same source. The *Liṅga-Purāṇa* (2,6, 6-7) in referring to the churning of the ocean says that *kālakūṭaviṣa,* the all-destroying cosmic poison came out first from the ocean; then out of that *Kālakūṭa* poison originated Jyeṣṭhā Devī, otherwise called Alakṣmī, who was very inauspicious. The *Padma Purāṇa*[12] contains three versions of the churning of the ocean (3, 9; 5, 4; and 6, 260). Out of these in the two versions only which describe the birth of Alakṣmī from the ocean the first thing to come out of the ocean is the *Kālakuṭa* and after *Kālakūṭa* was born Alakṣmī. According to the first version Alakṣmī when born had a black face, red eyes; she looked aged and she had dirty and tawny hairs on her head.[13] The second version depicts her as putting a red garment and decorated with garlands of red flowers

ज्येष्ठादेवी समुत्पन्ना
रक्तस्रक् वाससावृता। (*Padma,* p. 6.260.23)

and Lakṣmī was the eleventh entity to be produced. The *Liṅga Purāṇa* version[14] of the story traces the origin of Alakṣmī to the churning of the ocean no doubt, but the version differs a little. According to this text first came out the *Kālakūṭa* poison and from that *Kālakūṭa* poison was born Alakṣmī. Then after the birth of Alakṣmī was born Lakṣmī. Whereas in the *Padma Purāṇa* version Alakṣmī originated directly from the churning of the ocean, in the *Liṅga Purāṇa* after the *Kālakūṭa* poison came out Alakṣmī not directly from milky ocean but from the *Kālakūṭa* poison.

As we have noticed before, the origin of Lakṣmī from the churning of the ocean was never left out either by the authors of the Epics or by the redactors of the Purāṇas. The only development that one can trace by going through the story of the origin of Lakṣmī is that in the earlier versions Lakṣmī does not become the wife of Viṣṇu.[15] Neither Viṣṇu is anxious to get her as his wife. Only in later version[16] the relation of Viṣṇu with Lakṣmī has come up. Alakṣmī pictured as the elder sister of Lakṣmī had all the evil and inauspicious attributes in contradistinction from Lakṣmī who had been endowed with all the noble and auspicious qualities. But Alakṣmī was Jyeṣṭhā. She was born earlier. Once Lakṣmī the younger sister could be brought into union with Viṣṇu, it was impossible for the redactors of the Purāṇas to leave Alakṣmī alone without a mate (companion). In the earlier versions where Lakṣmī marries Viṣṇu, there is no mention of the origin of Alakṣmī. But once Alakṣmī was presented as originating earlier than Lakṣmī from the same milky ocean[17] and when following the earlier accounts Viṣṇu becomes anxious to accept her as his wife, Lakṣmī revolts against this custom of the marriage of the younger sister before the elder sister, which goes against the law books.[18] In the *Padma Purāṇa* (6,118, 4) when Viṣṇu is anxious to accept Lakṣmī as his wife, Lakṣmī puts up the objections–O Madhusūdana, how can it be possible for me to get married to you when my elder sister remains unmarried. So please get her married first, then only we shall marry.[19] Then Viṣṇu as *Padma Purāṇa* version continues, took note of the advice of Lakṣmī and got her elder sister Alakṣmī married to Uddālaka.

Here the *Purāṇakāra* by bringing together the union of Alakṣmī with Uddālaka, a woman having all the devilish qualities and a reputed sage having all the heavenly virtues has depicted the family feud in the most interesting and humorous manner.

Alakṣmī the personification of everything unholy and unrighteous shows the least regard for her husband. She hates everything what her husband likes. She hates to live in her husband's hermitage, made fragrant by sacrifices and resounding with the chanting of the Vedic *mantras*. She expresses her desire to her husband to take her to a place where everything is inauspicious and evil[20]. Then roaming about here and there in search of a suitable place for Alakṣmī Uddālaka assigned her a temporary residence in the Aśvattha tree and vanished.

The poor Alakṣmī after long waiting for Uddālaka got tired and wept bitterly. Then on the advice of his wife Viṣṇu came with his wife Lakṣmī to Aśvattha tree and consoled her with the words-O, Alakṣmī, let this Aśvattha tree a part and parcel of my ownself be your permanent abode. Your younger sister Lakṣmī will be coming to reside here only on Saturday. So on every Saturday the Aśvattha tree must be worshipped; but O Alakṣmī those who worship you everyday here, Lakṣmī will continue to live permanently with those house-holders.

Through this anecdote the *Purāṇakāra* found a clever device for popularising the worship of Aśvattha tree. By making the Aśvattha tree both the abode of Alakṣmī and Lakṣmī (only on Saturday) one could be able to pacify and propitiate the evil and through that one could be able to get the blessings of the other through the worship of Aśvattha tree. Since the Vedic age Aśvattha tree has attained significance and importance.

In the *Yajur Veda* (3.4.8.) Aśvattha tree is the residence of Gandharvas and Apsarasas. The *Atharvaveda* (3, 6, 5) prescribes the use of amulet of Aśvattha for entrapping the enemies and bringing them under control. In order to get relief from demons and to kill one's rivals, along with the wood of the Kṛkaṭasa tree the wood of the Aśvattha tree was added to the sacrificial fire (A.V. 2, 18, 1-5). For terrifying one's enemy the *Samidhas* of the Aśvattha tree were offered in the sacrificial fire (A.V. 88, 3). Even the branches of Aśvattha magically charmed by the Brahmin had the potency of driving away enemies in the battle field (A.V. 3, 6, 8).

The Gṛhya Sūtras connect the Aśvattha tree with different deities. In the *Gobhila Gṛhya Sūtra* (4, 7, 22) Aśvattha is sacred to the Sungod. In the *Mahābhārata* (13, 4, 27, ff) there is reference to the story of the mothers of Viśvāmitra and Jamadagni as to how they were blessed with sons by embracing Aśvattha and Udumbara. The tree is believed to be the seat of the dead ancestors (*V.S.* 25,4; *S.B.* 13, 8, 3, 1). So by worshipping the Aśvattha tree it was thought that the dead ancestors were honoured. The *Bhagavad-Gītā* (10, 26) gives an exalted position to the Aśvattha tree–

अश्वत्थ सर्व वृक्षाणां

The *Brahma Purāṇa* identifies Viṣṇu with this tree (Ch. 103,5). And at last here in the *Padma Purāṇa* Jyeṣṭhā and Lakṣmī both are brought into relation with the Aśvattha tree. The tree which had the potency of making the women fruitful is here pictured as the tree of plenty and prosperity. By worshipping this tree one is able to honour both Lakṣmī and Alakṣmī because it is the abode of both these deities.

The *Liṅga Purāṇa* version (2.6) of the chapter entitled Alakṣmī vṛtta makes Duḥsaha the husband of Alakṣmī. Like Uddālaka of the *Padma Purāṇa* Duḥsaha finds it difficult to pull on with his spouse. It is because Alakṣmī hates to listen to the chanting of Vedic *mantras* or recitation of the glory of Hara or Hari. The sage Duḥsaha in the meantime meets Mārkaṇḍeya. He puts the problem before him, the trouble he has faced because of the dirty habits of his wife. Then Mārkaṇḍeya gives him a long list of unholy and inauspicious places which are suitable for the residence of Alakṣmī.

Among the places described as worthy of residence of Alakṣmī are the homes where the preceptor and the guests are offended, where there is constant feud between the wife and husband, where neither Śiva nor Viṣṇu is worshipped, where people are bereft of good conduct, etc. On the whole anything that goes against the sacred laws of our law-makers is favourite of "Alakṣmī. It seems after Alakṣmī, the goddess of poverty and misfortune rose to pre-eminence, the redactor of *Liṅga Purāṇa* (2, 6, 31-74a) in describing the worthy places of Alakṣmī tried to connect her with those traits and characteristics which according to the Hindu mind are responsible for bringing poverty and misfortune.

When Mārkaṇḍeya after pointing out the places fit for Alakṣmī disappeared, Duḥsaha took his wife to those unholy places and specially to the hermitage where people were engaged in reviling Viṣṇu.

विष्णोः निन्दारतात्मनां (V. 76). In that hermitage resounding with calumny of Viṣṇu, Duḥsaha left her, and he himself entered the nether region not to be seen again.

As in the *Padma Purāṇa* version here also Alakṣmī left stranded in the hermitage of the revilers of Viṣṇu, complains of her pitiable plight to Viṣṇu. And Viṣṇu for her livelihood apportions to her the residence, the wealth and property, the land and the religious merits of those people who revile Brahmā, Viṣṇu and Śiva.

The *Mārkaṇḍeya Purāṇa* (50, 33ff) gives a different turn to the story. In place of Uddālaka of *Padma Purāṇa*, Duḥsaha of *Liṅga Purāṇa*, here Mṛtyu[21] (Death) becomes the husband of Alakṣmī. Nirṛti appears as the co-wife of Alakṣmī. Alakṣmī gives birth to fourteen sons who are ready to carry out the command of their father, Mṛtyu. Duḥsaha is the foremost among the sons of Alakṣmī. Like Alakṣmī represented as a conglomoration of every thing evil and inauspicious, her son Duḥsaha is portrayed as always living with unrighteous persons, influencing the people to be more passionate, more angry. In conformity with his nature Duḥsaha is pictured as naked, clothed in rags and having a voice hoarse as a crow's. He is always overtaken by hunger and in consequence he is ready to devour the whole universe.

At last Brahmā comes and requests Duḥsaha to be calm and free from passion. When Duḥsaha asks Brahmā to tell him his place of refuge and the method of satisfying his hunger and thirst, Brahmā allots to him those places which were very much aspired by her mother Alakṣmī. In the *Liṅga Purāṇa* Duḥsaha is ordered by Brahmā to remain with the unrighteous people who do not perform sacrifices and other ceremonies, who delight in gambling and women, and who are religious hypocrites. And his food is prescribed to be the remains of a meal, anything uncooked or badly cooked, anything polluted or cooked in broken pots etc.

Duḥsaha of *Liṅga Purāṇa* who was a great sage, who had great liking for the recitation of Hari and Hara and the chanting of the *mantras* of the Vedas, had great disappointment to get as wife Alakṣmī endowed with everything ignoble and vicious. But here in *Mārkaṇḍeya Purāṇa*, Alakṣmī is connected with a husband Mṛtyu having all the evil characteristics as his wife. And Duḥsaha becomes the son of Mṛtyu begot by Alakṣmī. Keeping in view of the vicious qualities of both the father and the mother, the son Duḥsaha has been pictured as the embodiment of everything devilish. Like Alakṣmī in *Padma Purāṇa* (6, 260, 25ff) and *Liṅga Purāṇa* (2, 16, 17 ff) the residence of religious and virtuous people, the worship of divinities, pure and holy conduct become intolerable for *Duḥsaha.*[22]

5. Worship of Alakṣmī a sine qua non for Attainment of Lakṣmī

Once Alakṣmī became famous for creating poverty and misfortune when she rose into prominence as an independent goddess representing everything evil, it was thought necessary to propitiate her and to appease her so that she may not exert her influence and bring poverty and misery to the people. In the annals of worship it is found that those deities who are malignant by nature and create troubles are generally worshipped (Frazer). In the *ṚgVeda* the Aryan was very much afraid of the fierce and destructive character of Rudra. He is implored not to slay or injure his worshippers. To avert his great malevolence[23] he is always prayed to be merciful. In the Purāṇa literature we notice that Skanda[24] with his four transformations was the lord or presiding deity of the Grahas i.e. asterisms causing suffering to children. These asterisms known as Skanda grahas exercise their evil influence in the life of a child. The only way to get rid of their evil influence was to give *bali*, offering, to them. Many ceremonies observed in honour of Yama[25] the god of death testify that the divinities famous for creating troubles or famous for creating mischief always get the highest honour. The worship of Gaṇeśa 'lord of troubles', Vighneśa 'disturber of peace' at the beginning of each and every ceremony points to the fact that it was always thought proper to placate him so that there should not be any interference in religious ceremonies.[26] The instance of the goddess Ṣaṣṭhī, sylvan deity accustomed to live in hills (classed under demons and spirits–E.R.E. IV. p 602) may be taken; she was primarily responsible for causing disease and taking away the life of the mother and child.[27] Primarily her worship was introduced to appease her, though later on she has adopted auspicious nature and has been represented as the giver and protector of children[28] (*Viṣṇudharmottara Purāṇa* 2,52,56). That is why in *Harśacarita*[29] and *Kādambarī*[30] she is called Jātahāriṇi and Bahuputrikā. Like Ṣaṣṭhī whose malignant nature has so to say been completely overshadowed by all the auspicious traits like protecting children, giving child to childless etc., another Hindu folk-goddess Hāritī,[31] now worshipped in Northern India as the protectress of children was originally a Yakṣiṇī, an ogress, a cannibal demon, who once devoured all the children in Rājagṛha. In the same line the worship of Alakṣmī came to be a regular feature in Hinduism. The only reason for her worship was to placate and propitiate her.[32]

6. Vratas for Warding off Alakṣmī

It is well-known fact that *Vratas* occupy the most important position in Hinduism. Most of the *Vratas* practised are *Kāmyā,* that performed for the purpose of securing some result in this world or sometimes in the other world or both. Many of these *Vratas* are really secular though under the garb of religion. And though certain disciplines (fast, worship, etc.) have to be observed, yet most of these *Vratas* breathe frankly a materialistic attitude. As heaven and liberation were the things most desired for making the after-life happy alongwith progeny, virtues and fame and learning, wealth or fortune was the most essential thing to make one's life in this world happy and cheerful. Therefore, we notice that many rites and ceremonies are observed in honour of Lakṣmī.[33] But as without propitiation of Alakṣmī it was difficult to attain Lakṣmī, many *Vratas* are referred to in the Gṛhya Sūtras and the Purāṇa literature refers to many *Vratas* in honour of Alakṣmī.

The *Baudhāyana Gṛhya Sūtra* dedicates a full chapter on Jyeṣṭhākalpa for the worship of Alakṣmī called Jyeṣṭhā. The *Vrata* is generally observed in the Prauṣṭhapada (Bhādrapada) in the Anurādhā *nakṣatra.* On such occasion offerings like til oil, *pāyasa, curd saktu, lājā,* rice-gruel and black clothes are offered. In the sacrifice for Jyeṣṭhā, til oil is offered as oblations to Indra, Jyeṣṭhā and Prajāpati. She is identified with Satyā, Kapliapatnī, Kumbhī, Varadā Hastimukhī, Vighnapārśadā, Prakumbhī etc.

The *Vrata* in honour of Jyeṣṭhā called Jyeṣṭhā *Vrata* described in *Liṅga Purāṇā* and *Skanda Purāṇa* has been quoted in Hemādri (II, 2.pp. 630-633) and *Nirṇaya Sindhu* (II. 6, 34). This Jyeṣṭhā Vrata (also called Nakṣatra Vrata) is to be observed by females on the eight day of the bright half of the month of Bhādrapada, if it is in conjunction with Jyeṣṭhā *nakṣatra.*[34] On this day worship of Jyeṣṭhā Devī (identified with Lakṣmī and Umā) is recommended for removal of Alakṣmī—

अलक्ष्मी विनिवृत्तये

Only women are entitled to perform her worship. Here the offerings prescribed for Jyeṣṭhā are wheat, barley, rice, and such other things. By propitiating Jyeṣṭhā females are in a position to remove barrenness, the defect of having only one child—

काकवन्ध्यादिदोष and poverty दारिद्र्य विनाशाय

She is worshipped by gods, demons, human beings and if pleased she bestows wealth and offspring. One should observe

Jyeṣṭhā *Vrata,* because like salt dissolving in water all the troubles of the devotees vanish for ever—

विघ्नास्तस्य प्रणश्यन्ति यथाप्सु लवणं तथा

Besides, Hemādri Vṛatakhaṇḍa (II. 638-640) quotes from *Bhaviṣyoṭtara Purāṇa* and presribes that the Jyeṣṭhā *vrata* can be observed on any *tithi* of the bright half of Bhādrapada when there is jyeṣṭhā *nakṣatra*. The *Vrata* can be observed by a woman whose children are dead or who has only one child and by a poor man. The *Vrata* can be observed continuously for twelve years or for the whole life. The image of Jyeṣṭhā Devī is to be worshipped and the devotee has to keep awake the whole night.

7. Alakṣmīnāśaka Snāna

Since the days of the Brāhmaṇas it is noticed that water has played a significant role in all the rites and ceremonies. In prescribing regular bath for the sacrificer and his wife it is only intended to remove the physical impurity. Besides, for warding off demons and goblins, water was invariably used—

आपो हि वै रक्षोघ्नी (T.B. 3.2.3.12)

Among the different rites necessary for removal of evil effects or their appeasement the Gṛhya Sūtra (*Baudhāyana Gr. S.* I. 14) recommends *udakaśānti* for mitigating all the troubles caused by the unfavourable position of the planets, for removing the impurity on birth or death in one's family. The *Bṛhat Saṁhitā* 47 (1-87), *Atharvāṇa pariśiṣtha* (V. pp. 66-68) *Viṣṇudharmottara Purāṇa* (2, 103, 30) refer to a type of *udakaśānti* called Puṣyā-śānti for the king for destroying all evil portents. "Water is indeed thunderbolt, he strikes the thunder bolt against enemies". Waters are destroyer of malignant spirits (and it is taken) for destroying evil spirits[35].

The eulogy of a bath in the Ganges or other big rivers like Kṛṣṇā, Godāvarī and Narmadā lies on this aspect of washing off the impurities of both body and mind. Similarity in later digests and commentaries like *Smṛti Kaustubha* (344-345), *Puruṣārtha*

Cintāmaṇi (307) and *Kālasāra* (178) a particular *snāna* called *Alakṣmī nāśakasnāna* is prescribed. On full-moon day of Pauṣa where there is Puṣyā *nakṣatra,* persons should bathe after anointing their bodies with white mustard and drive off Alakṣmī (Misfortune or poverty) and worship images of Nārāyaṇa, Indra, Moon, Bṛhaspati and Puṣya by bathing them in the water in which *Sarvauṣadhis* are put; and also he should perform *homa* in honour of these deities. The *Brahma Purāṇa* (Ch. 137) speaks of the river Ganges as Lakṣmītīrtha. In order to glorify the river Ganges[36] as having the potency of driving off Alakṣmī and endowing one with Lakṣmī the redactor of the Purāṇa depicts a story of quarrel between Lakṣmī and Daridrā (the same as Alakṣmī). Each of them claims one's own superiority; and at last they go to the river Ganges who gives her verdict in favour of Lakṣmī. Since then a bath in the river Ganges is recommended for *Alakṣmīnāśana* and to make oneself *Lakṣmīvān.*[37]

For warding off the evil effects and misfortune we have noticed before how prayers and presents were lavished upon Alakṣmī. Even in Jyeṣṭhā *Vrata* one can notice that Alakṣmī has been lauded as Lakṣmī and Umā (*tvam Lakṣmī tvam Uṃā devī*). But besides this propitiation and placation of evil spirits for making oneself free from their malignant influence the method of forcible expulsion was also adopted. For banishing the demons of epidemics like cholera and smallpox in Australia, South Africa, Malanesia, China and in our country India, people resort to different methods whenever any calamity befalls.[38] But sometimes the expulsion of evils tends to become periodic. It is thought to be desirable to have a general riddance of evil spirits at fixed times, usually once a year in order that people make a fresh start in life, freed from all malignant influences which have been accumulating about them.

This periodic expulsion of evil generally took place in the rainy season and in the agricultural season. Because with the first rains there was generally much sickness. In many countries the expulsion was resorted to when the rains begin.[39] At seed time the Khonds of India carry a basket containing each kind of seed donated by the people of the tribe. The basket containing the seeds is taken to a field outside the village by the chief priest of tribe. The seed thus carried out is called the share of the 'evil spirit, spoilers of the seed'. Thus being driven out with the car the evil spirits do not have any excuse for interfering with the rest of the seed corn[40]. But in some other cases the annul expulsion of devils takes place at harvest time instead of at seed time. At Kiriwina in South Eastern New Guina when the new jams have been harvested, people feast and dance for many days. When the festivities are over, all the people gather together and expel the devils from the village by shouting and beating the posts of the house.[41] The Hos of North Eastern India expel the demons after they have collected the harvest[42]. Among some of Hindookush tribes the expulsion of devils takes place after harvest. When the last crop of autumn has been got in, it is thought necessary to drive away evil-spirits from the granaries. The expulsion of Alakṣ mī (Goddess of poverty and misfortune) as referred to in the Purāṇa literature takes place in the harvesting season. The Dīpāvalī festival also called Dīpālīkā (in colophon to Ch.140 of *Bhaviṣyottara Purāṇa*) which falls in the harvesting season spreads over about five days. The whole of festival comprises five principal items, spread over five days-on the thirteenth of the dark half of Āśvina (by the *Pūrṇimānta* reckoning) lighting of lamps in honour of Yama (*Yama-trayodaśī*) the celebration of Viṣṇu's victory over Narakāsura (*Naraka caturdaśī*), on the new moon day worship of Lakṣmī (*Dīpānvitā Lakṣmī pūjā*), on the first day of bright half of Āśvina, victory of Viṣṇu over Bali (*Balipratipadā*) and on the second day of the bright half of Āśvina, the exchange of brotherly and sisterly affection (*Bhātṛdvitīyā*). Out of these five days of the festival, on the newmoon day the day singled out for the worship of Lakṣmī the expulsion of Alakṣmī is to be carried out after performing the worship of Lakṣmī.[44] When midnight is past and people's eyes are heavy with approaching sleep, the women in the city should create great noise by beating winnowing baskets and drums and should drive out Alakṣmī from the courtyards of their houses.[45]

This custom referred to in the Purāṇa literature is still current among the Hindoos. Crooke[46] refers to this method of expelling Alakṣmī as he noticed in the Punjab. On the morning after Divali the eldest woman of the house takes a corn-sieve or a winnowing basket and broom, beats them in every corner of the house saying " god abide and poverty depart". The sieve is then carried out of the village towards north or east and is thrown away. It is believed that the article thus thrown away bears away with it the poverty and disaster of the house. In general this is the present version of the practice of expelling Alakṣmī referred to in the Purāṇas. In Gujarat[47] this custom of driving away Alakṣmī takes place on the first day of Kārttika which is their new-year's day. On the other hand, the Hindus of Monghyr in Bihar observe this custom on Bhūtacaturdaśī day i.e. on the fourteenth day of the dark fortnight of Kārttika. But their way of expulsion of Alakṣmī is somewhat different. They make an image of Alakṣmī in cowdung and drag her and humiliate her saying-*Lachmighar, dariddar bāhar,* J.N. Banerjea[48] refers to another form of this ritual very much in vogue in several districts of Bengal, where a *Kṣaṇikā* (temporary) image of Alakṣmī is made of cowdung and is worshipped on the newmoon night of Dīpīvalī, then this crude image is taken outside the house with the beating of the winnowing fan and discarded. Whatever may be the method of expelling Alakṣmī, the sound produced by beating winnowing fan is the regular feature every where.

Producing sound is always connected with the expulsion of evil. For expelling the demons of epidemic the Solomn Islanders of Bougainville straits blow conchshells, beat tins, shout and knock on the houses.[49] In Southern China to expel the demon of cholera 'gongs are beaten, guns are fired, crackers are hopped and demon-dispelling trumpets are blown.[50] When cholera breaks out in any Burmese Village, the people thump drums, blow trumpets, yell scream, beat floors, walls, tin pans, every thing to make a din, because they think this uproar to be very effective to drive away cholera demon.[51]

The Bhviṣya Purāṇa (12,43) refers to the custom of attaching bells to the ears of the cattle for the sake of decoration and also for driving off the evil spirit.

घंटा: कर्णेषु बध्नियु: शोभा रक्षार्थमेव च।

The ringing of a bell at the appearance of dawn is recommended in the *Māhābhārata* (12, 48, 20), *Manusmṛti* (10, 33), where two different motives can be attributed-one is for driving off the evil spirits and the other is to invigorate the auspicious power–the newly rising Sun-

घंटा ताड़: अरुणोदये

Though in churches the ringing of bells at funerals is interpreted as a call to the faithful to pray for the departed soul, yet its original motive may be the supposed power of driving away evil spirits lying in wait for the dying man's soul. During the middle ages in Europe bells were chiefly valued for their prophylactic power in scaring the evil spirits from doing harm ghostly and bodily.[52] The Buddhists are also known to have resorted to the ringing of bells to expel the death demon. Therefore, when in place of propitiation and placation of such a malignant deity was not effective, the other means adopted was to ask her to go away. She was threatened and scared off from the house. That is why the *Purāṇakāras* recommend that a great sound should be produced by the beating of drums and winnowing baskets at the time of expelling Alakṣmī.

The beating of drums is not something uncommon for producing a sound but the sound produced by beating the winnowing fan (śūrpa) needs some explanation. Besides, being an emblem of increase and prosperity the winnowing fan has been regarded as possessing magical powers. Among the Kols, when a vacancy occurs in the office of the village priest, the winnowing fan with some rice is used, and by its magical power it drags the person who holds it towards the individual on whom the sacred mantle has fallen. The same custom prevails among the Oraons. As in India at present in Europe, too, divination is performed with a pair of shears and a winnowing fan. 'The shears are stuck in cornsieve or winnowing basket and the maidens hold up the sieve with the tip of their fingers by the handle of the shears, they say 'By St. Peter and St. Paul, he hath not stolen it.'[53] After many adjurations the sieve turns at the name of the thief. Even at present in our country this method of divination by rotating the winnowing fan is still prevalent. It is recommended[54] that a man if taken possession of troublesome spirits-the Vināyakas, one has to perform a rite in which offerings put in a winnowing fan are to be placed where four roads meet–

दद्यात् चतुष्पथे शूर्पे।

In Combodia certain evil spirits accept the offering provided the offering is brought to them in a winnowing basket.[55] The winnowing fan in which the corn is tossed and by means of which the chaff is blown utterly away was to Clement of Alexandria the symbol of utter ruin and destruction. The Egyptians used to burn their scape-goats alive, and their ashes they made away with by winnowing and scattering them.[56] From all these parallel instances cited above, the use of the winnowing fan an instrument endowed with magical powers for driving off the evil spirits, the nature of Alakṣmī becomes clear.

Like the winnowing fan the broom used for driving off Alakṣmī is equally endowed with magical potency. For warding off the evil eye the custom of striking the ground with a broom is well-known. Among Bani Israils[57] of Bombay when the midwife drives off the blast of the evil eye she holds in her left hand a shoe, a winnowing fan and a broom. Among the Mirzapur Korwas when a dust-storm comes, the women thrust the house broom, which is a demon-scarer, into the thatch, so that it may not be blown away. Even now the custom of putting the broom near the bed of the child is found where the sole reason is to ward off the evil spirits.[58]

Then we come to the question of the time of expulsion of Alakṣmī. Why does this expulsion occur on the new-moon day of Āśvina–after the worship of Lakṣmī, goddess of corn? The autumn season consisting of Bhādrapada and Āśvina is the harvesting season for *Bhādvi* crops. The cultivator is busy in the reaping and gathering of corn of various kinds. After the gathering in of various harvests all the deities and cornspirits are offered the first fruits of the year. If we look to the Hindu calendar, we notice that all the deities worshipped in this season are somehow or other related to corn. In the month of Bhādrapada on the third day of the bright half seven different varieties of corn are to be put in a winnowing fan; the seven types of corn are taken as the embodiment of the corn goddess Gaurī–

शूर्प प्ररूढ़ा नवसस्यमयीं *Bhaviṣyottara Purāṇa* (28. 58)

Then comes the celebration of Durgā Pūjā continuing from the first to the ninth day in the bright half of Āśvina. The Goddess Durgā is but a vegetation spirit or corn-mother. This aspect of the deity is evident in her epithet Śākambharī.[59] Then again the new-moon day of Āśvina is very important day for the worship of Lakṣmī, the corn-goddess. The same deity is worshipped alongwith Indra riding Airāvata on the full-moon day of Āśvina; the festival is famous as *Kaumudimahotsava.* The explanation of the worship of these corn-goddesses like Lakṣmī and Gaurī at this particular period[60] lies in fact that these two months-Bhādrapada and Āśvina are important for harvest-home; hence the worship of the corn mothers. After the harvest-home one can notice the *Navānnabhakṣaṇa*-partaking of the fresh crops in Mārgaśirṣa. Naturally therefore the day of Dīpāvali was selected for driving off Alakṣmī, as by this time one was strengthened and fortified oneself by the advent of fresh crops–Lakṣmī incarnate. Presence of Lakṣmī–the newly harvested crop gave sufficient encouragement to throw off Alakṣmī (bad luck, penury, poverty, ill-luck) from one's home and courtyard. Among the Hos of North-Eastern India after the celebration of the great festival-the harvest-home when the granaries are full, women and children go in procession in every part of the village with sticks in their hands to drive off the evil-spirit. Among the Hos and Mundaris when the last crop of autumn has been got in, it is thought necessary to drive away evil spirits from the granaries.[61]

8. Iconographical Representation of Alakṣmī

Lakṣmī, Goddess of fortune or wealth primarily represented goddess of ripe-corn. In the harvesting season the agricultural community places a corn-measure filled with ripecorn, adores it with flowers as the representative of Lakṣmī.[62] Naturally, therefore, iconographically Lakṣmī was represented as Gaurī and this Gauri is defined as–

रक्तपीत समायोगात् गौरी इत्यभिधीयते।

Nāṭyaśāstra (23,73)–that which is a mixture of red and yellow colour-is explained as *gaura*. This explanation of *gaura* conforms to the first variety of Gauri[63] as explained in *Viṣṇu-dharmottara Purāṇa*. The symbolical representation of Lakṣmī through ripe corn, the recommendation of *Viṣṇudharmottara Purāṇa* that the image of Lakṣmī should be of *gaura* (a mixture of red and yellow colour) helps us to see in Lakṣmī, the goddess of ripe corn.

Alakṣmī, the deity of misfortune and poverty who came to the picture later and who represented all the evil and inauspicious characteristics unlike the auspicious ones of Lakṣmī, iconographically came to be represented through images made of all types of unholy and inauspicious things. While the Śrī-Sūkta spoke of Lakṣmī as *hiraṇyavarṇā* having golden colour (reminding us of the colour of the ripe wheat or paddy), Alakṣmī image was recommended to be dark colour like ink.

According to the description of Alakṣmī (referred to as Jyeṣṭhā Devī as given in Aṁśumadbhedāgama, 49th Patala, quoted by Hemadri), she is a goddess with two arms and two eyes with big cheeks and large pendulous breasts descending as far as the navel, with a flabby belly, thick thighs, raised nose, hanging lower lips and colour as dark as ink. Her legs have to be hanging down in front of the Bhadrāsana in which she is seated. Her hair is done up in a knot and on the forehead a *tilaka* is marked. She wears a *makuṭa* on her head; in her right hand she holds a Nīlotpala flower, and the other hand rests upon the seat. One authority however states that she would carry a Nīlotpala in one hand and keep the other in the *abhaya* pose. In actual sculpture she is often seen with the right hand in the *abhaya* pose and the left hand made to rest upon her thigh. Sometimes in the sculptures the right hand holds the Nīlotpala flower and the left hand rests upon the seat.

The ugly features like big cheeks and large pendulous breasts, etc. referred to by Hemadri definitely indicate that the goddess has assimilated many non-Aryan aboriginal divinities with her. Gopinath Rao[64] gives a list of names of Jyeṣṭhā as given in the old Tamil *Nighantus*. They are Mugadi, Tauvi, Kalādi, Mudevi, Kettai. Like numerous village deities (*Grāma Devatā*) of the aboriginal population-Gaṅgāmmā, the goddess of small pox, Marāmmā the goddess of cholera, Kokkalāmmā, the goddess of cough, Sukhalāmmā the goddess of measles, Udalāmmā, the goddess of swollen necks, goddess Jyeṣṭhā has come to be associated with poverty and misfortune with which she is supposed to afflict mankind. The long hanging breasts are everywhere regarded as one of the most unsightly features in a woman's form. Firm upright breasts are characteristics of motherhood and symbols of fertility. That is why when *Matsya Purāṇa* describing the method of the image of Lakṣmī says that the image of Lakṣmī should be *pīnonnatastanataṭā, raktoṣṭhī, pīnagaṇḍā.*[65] Alakṣmī's image is to be (*lambamānastanā, lamboṣṭhā*), large pendulous breasts and hanging lower lip.

Lakṣmī originally a corn-goddess later came to represent not only prosperity in grains, but prosperity in every walk of life. That is why the different concepts like Rājalakṣmī, Jayalakṣmī, Vīralakṣmī, etc. Likewise Alakṣmī came to be regarded in course of time not only as absence of wealth-penury or poverty but it came to signify every thing inauspicious and evil. Therefore, in contrast to Lakṣmī who came to be regarded as not only a goddess of fortune but as the goddess of beauty, Alakṣmī developed not only as a goddess of misfortune or ill-luck but as a goddess, symbolising an embodiment of all inauspicious features.

As Lakṣmī became the goddess of prosperity in every sphere of life, those things which are auspicious are related to her like elephant, lotus etc. Similarly Alakṣmī who is pictured as the embodiment of an evil spirit, goddess of ill-luck and poverty, ass was put as her *vāhana* (carrier) *kharārūḍhā*. As the carrier of Alakṣmī is regarded to be so much inauspicious that even if seen in a dream, is believed to cause the downfall or death of the person seeing it.[67] If its flesh is taken by a Brahmin, he had to undergo a severe penance of *Taptakṛchra* for the atonement of such sin.[68] Similarly if a Sūdra, or a Vaiśya or a Kṣatriya commits adultery with a higher caste woman, the woman so adulterated is made naked and her head being shaved and her body being anointed with butter, she is made to sit on a donkey and conducted along the high road for the atonement of the sin.[69] The ass which is looked upon as an inauspicious or ominous animal is fittingly selected to be the carrier of Alakṣmī, the goddess of misfortune and proverty.

The carrier of Jyeṣṭhā reminds us of another folk goddess Śītalā, goddess of small-pox who is of malignant nature. Śītalā rides on a donkey, has such emblems as sweeping broom and pitcher, and is adorned with a winnowing fan on her head.[70] Jyeṣṭhā who was once so popular deity in South India has now became practically obsolete. But the ground lost by Jyeṣṭhā in her home land was gained by her under another name, Śītalā in eastern and western parts of India: Bengal, Orissa, Gujarat etc.

Apart from this carrier ass, *Baudhāyana Gṛhya Sūtra*[71] while describing Jyeṣṭhā Vrata suggests carriers like lion and tiger in her chariot in Jyeṣṭhā's *dhyāna mantra*[72]–lions are attached to her chariot and tigers follow her.

These carriers show her identification with Durgā who has lion as her carrier. As has been pointed out, Alakṣmī is addressed as Umā and Lakṣmī. The *dhyāna mantra* of Durgā

(तामग्निवर्णां तपसा ज्वलन्ती शरणं अहं प्रपद्ये)

which is used in the worship of Alakṣmī *corroborates* the same.

The Sum up : Lakṣmī who was primarily a corn-goddess when merged with Śrī, the Vedic goddess of beauty and brilliance, represented not only as goddess of corn but also the goddess of beauty and well-being. Gradually when she rose to eminence, she stood not as a deity of corn only but became a deity representing whole human fortune and wellbeing. When Lakṣmī became established as the goddess of wealth, well-being and prosperity, another deity namely Alakṣmī appeared to represent the other side of human fortune-poverty, misery, misfortune, calamity, etc. When one is in a state of prosperity, such state is attributed due to the favour and grace of the goddess Lakṣmī; but the state of poverty, ill-luck or disaster is taken to be the influence of Alakṣ mī, the goddess of ill-luck and poverty. The state of disaster or destruction is taken to be due to the advent of Alakṣmī or her malignance.

In the *Mahābhārata* (3, 94, 10 ff) the prosperity of Gods is believed to be due to the favour of Lakṣmī, the goddess of prosperity; but the utter destruction and ruin of the demons was attributed to the evil influence of Alakṣmī, the goddess of misfortune. Gradually Alakṣmī became the embodiment of all the evil features-misfortune, disaster and distress. The sad plight of Rāma who was exiled from his kingdom without being coronated, and the loss of Sītā as well as Jaṭāyu in the forest, was attributed to the evil influence of this inauspicious deity, Alakṣmī.[73] She was taken to be so much terrible and dangerous to the society that she was thought to dry the ocean and extinguish fire when furious. So people were terribly afraid of such a malignant deity. All the misfortune, ill-luck, ruin or destruction in one's life is generally thought to be due to the influence of Alakṣmī, the goddess of ill-luck. So generally Alakṣmī is adored by the people for fear of her terrible influence.

References

1. Depending upon the interpretation of the word '*Vṛṣadaṁśa' as biḍāla* in V.S. (24, 31), Geldner takes the meaning of the word vṛṣadatī in verse 4 of this hymn as referring to a female cat. Accordingly he

interprets the whole hymn as referring to a cat. Because the cat owing to its peculiar features appears as a witch, and because in popular belief cats and witches are always connected, Geldner is inclined to see in this hymn a reference to the cat, a symbol of the witch. Pischel UND Geldner, *Vedische Studien*-Von., pp. 313-315.

2. Ṛg*Veda* (with commt. of Sāyaṇa) Vol. IV, Preface, pp. 901-2.
3. Scheftelowitz, 'Srī Sukta', *ZDMG*, p. 38
4. क्षुत्पिपासामलां ज्येष्ठां ष्ठां ष् + ठ = ष्ठ + आ = ष्ठा
अलक्ष्मीर् नाशयाम्यहम्।
अभूतिमसमृद्धिं च
सर्वां निर नुद मे गृहात्। (V. 8)
5. आदित्यवर्णे तपसोऽधिजातो
वनस्पतिस्तव वृक्षोऽथ विल्वः।
तस्य फलानि तपसा नुदन्तु
या अन्तरा याश्च बाह्या अलक्ष्मीः।। (Srī Sūkta, Verse 6)
6. M. Winternitz, *History of Indian Literature,* Vol. I, part I, p. 171 ff.
7. W. Kirfel, *Das Purāṇa Pañcalakṣaṇa,* Introduction, pp. IX-X.
8. *Ibid.*, p. 37.
9. *Ibid.*, p. 41.
10. For a comparative study of the Legend See *Purāṇa* Journal, Vol. IX, No. 1, January 1967, pp. 7-61.
11. उत्पादनार्थं लक्ष्म्याश्च–*Padma Purāṇa* 6.260.6; *Padma,* p. 5.4; *Viṣṇu,* p. 1-9.
12. *Padma Purāṇa,* 6, 260; 5,4; 3,9;
13. ततः अलक्ष्मीः विभ्रर्ति तनुं (Padma. p. 3.9.9)
14. *Linga* p. 2.6, 6-7.
ज्येष्ठा तेन समाख्याता अलक्ष्मीर्द्विजसत्तमः।
अमृतोद्भव वेलायां विषानान्तरं उल्वणात्।।6।।
अशुभा सा तथोत्पन्ना ज्येष्ठा इति च वै श्रुतम्।
ततः श्रीश्च समुत्पन्ना पद्मा विष्णु परिग्रह।।7।।
15. *Mbh. Cr. Edn.* 1, 17, 36
श्री सुरा चैव सोमश्च तुरगश्च मनोजवः।
यतो देवाः ततो जग्मुर् आदित्यपथमाश्रितः।।36।।
16. Matsya, p. 250-3
जग्राह कमलां विष्णुः

17. *Liṅga* p. 2, 6; *Padma* p. 6, 260.

18. *Baudh. D.S. 2,1.39; Manusmṛti 3,172.*

19. असंस्कृत्य कथं ज्येष्ठा कनिष्ठा परिणीयते।
तस्मात् ममाग्रजा एतां अलक्ष्मीं मधुसूदन।।
विवाह्य नय मां पश्चात् एष धर्मः सनातनः।। (*Padma,* P. 6.118.4)

20. The choice of Alakṣmī rests with a residence where there is constant family feud, where the guests are not honoured, where the thieves and scoundrels are in plenty, where people take recourse to illicit love, in other words whatever has been proscribed by law makers like Manu, Yājñavalkya have been portrayed as the most cherished thing for Alakṣmī (*Padma* P. 5, 118-12-16).

21. Prof. Kirfel in his introduction to *Purāṇa Pañcalakṣaṇa* very aptly remarks-in the process of the development of Purāṇa Litera- ture many co-workers have come to the field as a result it has been difficult to arrange the subject matter. Sometimes an individual has himself composed the entire text, or sometimes he is only a redactor, who gathers the text already existing, who arranges and who turns the text into a connected whole through his own contribution, expansion and revision. Because of this we notice such divergent descriptions in the Purāṇa literature. In one version, Uddālaka becomes the husband of Alakṣmī, another version makes Duḥsaha her husband; and in the third version Mṛtyu is the husband of Alakṣmī and Duḥsaha is her son.

22. *Mārkaṇḍeya Purāṇa, 50, 33 ff.*
According to Eliot 'the evil spirit Duḥsaha described in the Mārkaṇḍeya Purāṇa comes very near the Devil', *Hinduism and Buddhism,* Vol. I, Introduction, LXXIX Note 1.

23. A. Macdonell, *Vedic Mythology,* p. 75.

24. *Vāyu* P., 72, 24ff; *Brahmāṇḍa* P. 2.55; 3, 11; *Liṅga P.,* 1, 104, 105; *Matsya P.* 6, 26ff; 3,146-160; *Śiva P.* Chs. 9-19; *Vāmana P.* Ch. 57& 58; *Padma P.* 6, 28; *Skanda P.* I, 1.20-30, I, 2, 20-32.

25. (*a*) *Yama caturthī*
(*b*) *Yama dīpadāna*
(*c*) *Yama tarpaṇa*
(*d*) *Yama dvitīyā*
(*e*) *Yama vrata*
(*f*) *Yama darśanatrayodaśī.*

26. *The Age of Imperial Unity,* p. 469.

27. (*a*) P.K. Agrawala. 'Skanda in the Purāṇās and Classical Literature', *Purāṇās* Vol. VIII, 1, Jan., 1966, 151ff. Saṣṭhī otherwise called Jātahāriṇī, assimilated in herself all the folk-goddesses concerning the diseases of the mother and the child.

    (*b*) A. Bhattacharya in his article 'The Cult of *Saṣṭhī* in Bengal' refers to an interesting folk tale signifying the malignant aspect of *Saṣṭhī,* A cat, the carrier of *Saṣṭhī* carries off the seven children of the youngest daughter-in-law, because of some defect in worship of *Saṣṭhī. Man in India,* Vol. XXVIII, 1948, pp. 152-162.
28. *Brahmavaivarta,* P. 2, 8, 10; *Devī Bhāgavata,* 9, 46.
29. *Harśacarita*. Ch. 4, 129.
30. *Kādambarī,* 64.
31. A. Getty, *The gods of Northern Buddhism* pp. 84-85; also see J.N. Banerjee, *The Development of Hindu Iconography,* pp. 380-81.
32. In this connection a very interesting stanza may be quoted from the *Mahābhārata* :

    अकृतोपद्रवः कश्चिन्महान् अपि न पूज्यते।
    पूजयन्ति नरा नागान् न तार्क्ष्यं नागघातिनम्।।6।।

    Mahābhārata, Vanaparva, 28, 16, Ed. T.R. Krishnamacharya and T.R. Vyasacharya, Bombay 1908. 'Inspite of all the glory and greatness one is never adored unless one is capable of creating trouble and mischief. People are so much zealous in worshipping the serpents; but they are callous towards Garuḍa, the killer of serpents.'
33. (*a*) *Aśunyaśayana Dvitīyā*
    (*b*) *Viśokadvādaśī*
    (*c*) *Kojāgara Pūrṇimā*
    (*d*) *Dīpāvalī*
    (*e*) *Śrīpañcamī*, etc.
34. Provided there is a Sunday in addition to above, the deity adored is Nīla Jyeṣṭhā.
35. *Vidh.* P. 2, 103, 30.

    अलक्ष्मी शमनं पुण्यं रक्षोघ्नं बुद्धि वर्धनम्।
    आरोग्यदं दीप्तिकरं यशस्य शत्रुसूदनम्।।
36. To most men in India like the Himalayas, the Ganges presents a double aspect-the physical aspect and the spiritual aspect. A great river apart from its volume of water is deemed to have a spiritual or divine life which animates it.

37. ततः प्रभृति तत् तीर्थं अलक्ष्मी नाशनं शुभम्।
    तत्र स्नानेन दानेन लक्ष्मीवान् पुण्यवान् भवेत्॥4॥

(*Brahma Purāṇa* 137, 41)

38. Sir J. Frazer, 'The occasional expulsion of 'Evil', *Golden Bough,* Vol. IX, pp. 106-123.
39. *Ibid.,* p. 128.
40. *Ibid.,* p. 133.
41. *Ibid.,* p. 134.
42. *Ibid.,* p. 136.
43. *Ibid.,* p. 137.
44. *Padma,* P. 6, 124.
45. एवं गते निशिथे तु
    जने निद्रान्धलोचने॥28॥
    तावत् नगरनारीभिः शूर्पडिंडिमवादनैः।
    निष्कास्यते प्रहृष्टाभिः अलक्ष्मीः स्वगृहांगनात्॥29॥

[*Padma* P. 6, 124, 28-29]

46. *Popular Religion and folk lore of Northern India.* Also quoted by Frazer, *Golden Bough* IX, p. 144 ff.
47. Stevenson, *The rites of the twice born,* p. 265.
48. *Loc. Cit.*
49. *Ibid.,* p. 116.
50. *Ibid.,* p. 117.
51. In two chapters of Frazer's Golden Bough, Vol. IX, Ch. III & IV, in describing the expulsion of evils either occasional or periodic, the expulsion of embodied evils, we can notice that noise or uproar is always connected with expulsion of evil.
52. E.R.E. VI. p. 315 ff.
53. Aubrey, Quoted in *Popular Religion and folk lore of Northern India,* Vol. II, pp. 187-190.
54. *Mānava Gr.*S. 2, 14, 30; *Yājñavalkya Smṛti* I. 285.
55. E.R.E. III. p. 153.
56. J. Harrison, *Prolegommena to the study of Greek Religion*, p. 104.
57. Crooke, *Popular Religion and Folklore of Northern India*, Vol. II, p. 190.
58. Crooke, *Ibid.,* Vol. I, p. 81.

59. (*a*) S.N. Kaviraj, 'Fertility Cult and tree'. *Tree symbol Worship in India,* pp. 148, 155.

(*b*) R.C. Hazara, Compilation of Purāṇic works or chapters on Sakti Worship', *Our Heritage*, Vol. IV, Part I, January-June 1956, pp. 67-98.

(*c*) ततोऽहं अखिलं
लोकं आत्मदेहसमुद्भवैः।
भरिष्यामि सुराशाकैः।
आवृष्टैर्प्राणिधारकैः।।43।।
शाकंभरीति विख्यांति
तदा यास्याम्यहं भुवि।।44a।। (*Mār*. P. 91, 43-44)

'Next O' Gods, I shall nourish the whole world with the life sustaining vegetables which shall grow out of my own body during a period of heavy rain. I shall gain fame on the earth then as 'Śākambharī'.

60. In Greece in the month of Thargelion, the later part of May and beginning of June, there was the grain harvest. So for the Greeks this month is marked by three important harvest festivals. Jane Harrison in Ch-III. 'Harvest festivals'–very nicely connects celebration of these festivals with reaping and garnering of the various kinds of cereals. pp. 77-119.

61. Frazer, *Golden Brought*, IX, pp. 137ff.

62. Todd. *Annals and antiquities of Rajasthan,* pp. 454-455. Even now in Orissa on every Thursday of the month of Mārgasīrsa, the custom of this type of worship is still prevalent.

63. *Vidh*. P. 3, 27, 11 ff.

गौरी पंचविधा तत्र श्यामा द्वादशधा भवेत्।।11।।
रुक्मगौरी दन्तगौरी स्फुटचन्दनगौर्यपि।
शरद्घनचन्द्रकवत् गौरी पञ्चविधा स्मृता।।12।।

'Among these colours, the gaurī (i.e. light shade) should be of five kinds...... Bright gold, light white, tooth-white, pure sandal white, autumn-cloud-white and autumn moon white-these five traditionally are called the five-fold Gaurī (light sha

64. T.A.G. Rao, *Elements of Hindu Iconography,* Vol. I, Part II. p. 395.

65. *Ibid.,* pp. 133-135.

66. *Ibid.,* p. 158.

67. *Rāmāyaṇa,* 5, 27, 19ff.

68. *Manusmṛti*, ii, 157.
69. *Vaśiṣṭha,* D.S. 21,1-5.
70. नमामि शीतलां देवीं रासभस्थां दिगम्बरीम्।
    मार्जनी कलसोपेतां शूर्पालंकृतमस्तकाम्।।
    Also quoted by J.N. Banerjee. *Development of Hindu Iconography,* p. 25.
71. Baudhāyana Gr. S., pp. 294-296.
72. यस्या: सिंहा: रथे युक्ता
    व्याघ्राश्चाप्यनुगामिन: [Baudh. Gṛ. S.]
73. Rām 3. 63, 20-23

    राज्यात् भ्रंशो वनवास: सीता नष्ट द्विजो हत:।।20।।
    ईदृशीयं ममालक्ष्मी: निर्दहेदपि पावकम्।
    सम्पूर्णं चेदद्य प्रतरेयं महोदधिम्।।21।।
    सोऽपि नूनं ममालक्ष्म्या विशुष्येत् सरितां पति:।।22a।।

CHAPTER 8

Prahlādaś Cāsmi Daityānām

Story of Prahlāda in the Bhāgavata Purāṇa

Each one of us is acquainted with the story of Prahlāda. As narrated in *Bhāgavata*, he was the son of Hiraṇyakaśipu, and he was a great devotee of Viṣṇu. And for that he was put to severe oppressions by his father Hiraṇyakaśipu who just could not tolerate to hear the glories of Viṣṇu. So the angry father tortures the innocent Prahlāda, the demon boy of five years old in very many ways. Demons strike him with deadly weapons; snakes bite him with their fangs; elephants of the quarters trample upon him; cooks supply him with deadly poison; magic spell is used against him; he is thrown down from lofty mountain peaks; but poor Prahlāda because of his utmost devotion to Viṣṇu survives all these tests. Then once Hiraṇyakaśipu challenges Prahlāda to show him his adorable Viṣṇu who is declared by Prahlāda to be present every where. In a state of fury the powerful demon strikes the nearest pillar with his fist to disprove the thesis of Prahlāda. All on a sudden Viṣṇu taking the terrible figure of man-lion (*nṛsiṁha*) appears out of that pillar to assert His omnipresence. And with his nails he tears Hiraṇyakaśipu to pieces. This is in short the story of Prahlāda narrated in detail in ten Chapters of the *Bhāgavata* (7th Book, Chapters 1-10). Beginning from the Vedic period the story of Prahlāda has undergone much change and modification; and at last he has appeared as a great devotee of Viṣṇu in the *Bhāgavata Purārṇa*, the holy book of the *Vaiṣṇavas*.

In the Vedic literature for the first time we come across Prahlāda in the *Taittirīya Brāhmaṇa* (1.5.9.1)[1]. Gods and demons are ready to fight. *Prajāpati* is anxious to protect the life of his eldest son Indra; so he takes him out of the battle-field, and hides him in a secret place, so that mighty demons would not be able to kill him. Similarly Prahlāda, the son of Kayādhu (*prahlāda ha vai kayādhavaḥ*)[1] anxious to protect the life of this son *Virocana* takes him out of the battle field, and hides him somewhere so that gods will not be able to kill Virocana. And both the armies of gods and demons are without their leaders.

The next mention of Prahlāda is in *Sāṁkhyāyana Āraṇyaka* (5.1). Indra kills the descendants of Prahlāda (*prahlādiyān*). In the *Kauṣitakī Upaniṣad* (3.1) the story runs that Pratardana has gone to Indra. Indra boasts of his vigour before Pratardana, and says that he has slain the hosts of Prahlāda. The only thing that becomes clear in all these references is that there is a fight between Indra and the descendants of Prahlāda, and the descendants of Prahlāda have been defeated or slain. This is not something uncommon in the Vedic literature, where many a time is presented the picture of the fight between gods and demons. The above narration brings out that in Vedic mythology Prahlāda was just a demon, and the name of his son was Virocana.

Next we come to the *Mahābhārata* and the Purāṇas. Except giving the name of the mother and the son of Prahlāda the Vedic literature is silent about his family line. But in *Mahābhārata* (1. 59. 16ff)[2] the genealogy of Prahlāda is given in detail. Unlike the gods born from Aditi all the demons were born from Diti. Diti through Kaśyapa gave birth to Hiraṇya-kasipu. Hiraṇya-kaśipu had five sons–Prahlāda, Saṁhlāda, Anuhlāda, Śivi and Vāṣkala. Prahlāda was the eldest of all. Prahlāda had three sons-Virocana, Kumbha and Nikumbha. Bali was the son of Virocana, and Bāṇa was the son of Bali.

It is well-known that in course of time through many redactions and recensions the Purāṇa literature has assumed a vast proportion. Prof. Kirfef in his '*Das Purāṇa Pañcalakṣaṇa*'.[3] has tried to arrive at the original Purāṇa literature by divesting it of its later additions and exaggerations. Following the very old definition that every Purāṇa is supposed to have five characteristics : (*i*) *sarga*-creation (*ii*) *pratisarga,* 're-creation', that is, the periodical annihilation and renewal of the worlds, (*iii*) *Vaṁśa*-genealogy of gods and sages, (*iv*) *Manvantarāṇi*-the great periods, each of which has a Manu or primal ancestor of the human race, (*v*) *Vaṁśānucarita*-the history of the dynasties, Prof. Kirfel has collated most of the Purāṇas, and has presented to us the old nucleus of the Purāṇa-literature. In the genealogical table preserved in the 'Purāṇa-pañca-lakṣaṇa' text Diti has two sons through Kaśyapa-Hiraṇyakaśipu and Hiraṇyākṣa. Hiraṇyakaśipu has four sons of great prowess (*vīryavān*)[4]–Anuhlāda, Hlāda, Prahlāda and Saṁhlāda (Kirfel. p. 165. verse 68 and 69, p. 215. verse 9). Of all these sons Prahlāda was the eldest (Kirfel. p. 196, verse 26). Thus the tradition regarding the genealogy of Prahlāda in the Purāṇas is maintained more or less in the same way as given in the *Mahābhārata*.

Then we come to examine his virtues and qualities as given in the epic and the Purāṇa texts. After Pṛthu was installed as the paramount lord, Brāhmā installed Varuṇa as the king of waters, Viṣṇu as the king of Ādityas. Then he made Prahlāda of incomparable energy the king of *Daityas* and *Dānavas* (Kirfel, p. 227, verse 5)[5]. As is natural with demons, Prahlāda along with his father and uncle (all designated as *dānavendras*) takes delight in all kinds of wicked acts. Prahlāda along with Hiraṇyakaśipu, Virocana and Bali go against the command of Brahmā, they transcend all restraints of duty and religion, they are responsible for destroying the cause of righteousness (*Mahābhārata* 12. 160. 26-28)[6]. As referred to in Vedic literature, Indra being a god had killed Prahlāda's descendants, who are demons. But in the *Mahābhārata* and the Purāṇas there is fight between Indra, lord of gods (*devendra*) and Prahlāda, lord of demons (*dānavendra*). This mythical fight between Indra and Prahlāda is referred to many a time, Indra's chariot is given to Arjuna for use, in that connection the poet of the *Mahābhārata* (3.165.18) refers to the great achievements that Indra has attained by making use of that chariot. "Along with Sambara, Vala, Vṛtra, Namuci and Naraka. Indra has defeated Prahlāda by using this chariot."[7] Indra takes pride in the fact that he has become the chief of gods (*devādhipa*)[8] after having killed in battle all the sons of Diti, Danu and also Prahlāda. Nobody can live in peace by being inimical to Indra. Along with other *dānavas* he has driven out Prahlāda from heaven[9]. This mythical fight between Indra and Prahlāda is given in 'Purāṇa-pañcalakṣana' texts with a little exaggeration.[10] The terrible fight between Indra and Prahlāda continued for three hundred years; yet there was no chance of victory for any one of them.[11] The fight took place at the time of churning of the ocean when Indra killed Prahlāda.[12]

This fierce and terrible fight between lords of two antagonistic races captured, the imagination of the author of the *Mahābhārata.* Whenever there is description of any duel, this fight of Indra and Prahlāda is used as a simile. The fight between Lakṣmaṇa and Indrajit was exceedingly wonderful like that between Indra and Prahlāda (*ativa citram āścaryam śakra-prahlādayoriva, Mahābhārata, 3.273.18*). The fight between Hanumān and the demon Dhūmrākṣa was fierce and terrible like that between Indra and Prahlāda (*tayoḥ yuddham abhūt ghoram indra-prahlādayoriva-Mahābhārata* 3.270.12). The fight between Aśvathāman and Ghaṭotkaca resembled the encounter between Indra and Prahlāda (*yuddham drauṇi-rākṣasayoḥ sakraprahlāda-yoriva, Mahābhārata* 7.141.28). The war between Karṇa and Ghaṭotkaca, both roaring against each other resembled that between Indra and Prahlāda (*Śakra-Prahlādayoriva-Mahābhārata*-7.148.62). When Bhīma killed Alambusa in battle, the Pāṇḍavas worshipped Bhīma just as Maruts worshipped Indra after he defeated Prahlāda in battle (*prahlādaṁ samare jitvā yathā śakraṁ marudgaṇāḥ-Mahābhārata,* 7.83.39). To the writer of the *Mahābhārata,* it seems the fight between Indra and Prahlāda was of great antiquity; so that fight of hoary past was always put as a model.

Other Aspects of the Character of Prahlāda

Besides being pictured as the lord of demons and as such engaged in fight with Indra, the lord of gods, there are other episodes in the *Mahābhārata* where Prahlāda is presented as an ideal hero sticking to truth and piety at all costs. Once Bali, his grand-son approaches him to know which is more meritorious-forgiveness (*kṣamā*) or might and energy (*tejas*). Prahlāda the chief of demons, possessed of great wisdom, well-versed in the mysteries of *dharma,* conversant with all conclusions (*mahāprāj-ña, dharmāṇām āgatāgamam, sarvaniścaya-vid, Mahābhārata,* 3.29.2, 3.29.5) gives detailed instructions indicating as to when one is to take recourse to forgiveness or might (*Mahābhārata,* 3.29.1-32).

Many times in the *Mahābhārata* (2.61,65-79; 5.35.21-30, 5.33.84) there is narrated a quarrel between *Virocana,* son of Prahlāda, and the *brahmin Sudhanvan*, son of *Aṅgiras*. Each of them is anxious to get *Keśinī* as his bride. Both of them at last come to Prahlāda as their arbitrator. At the sight of Sudhanvan, Prahlāda at once orders for water and *madhuparka* to worship Sudhanvan, because the latter happens to be a brahmin (*udakaṁ madhuparkaṁ cāpi ānayantu sudhanvane,* 5.35.20). In deciding the case Prahlāda gives his verdict in favour of the brahmin Sudhanvan and against his own son. Not only this, further addressing Virocana he says, "O Virocana, Sudhanvan is superior to you; his father Aṇgiras is superior to me; his mother is superior to your mother" (2.61.77–78. *Mahābhārata*). In grateful acknow-ledgment of the verdict given in his favour Sudhanvan says, 'O Prahlāda, unmoved by affection for thine own son thou hast adhered to virtue (*putra snehaṁ parityajya yastvam dharme pratisthitaḥ,* 2,61.79)". Thou hast preferred virtue, and hast not, from temptation said an untruth (*yad dharmam avṛnīthās tvam na kāmād aṇṛtam vadīh–5.35.30*).

Then we come to another episode in the *Mahābhārata* where Indra as a devoted disciple sits at the feet of Prahlāda, his spiritual teacher. It is said here (12.124) that Prahlāda by merit of his virtue and good conduct (*śila*) has snatched away the sovereignty of Indra, and has become the lord of three worlds. Divested of his power and fortune Indra comes to Bṛhaspati to know the source of supreme bliss. But not satisfied with the teachings of

Bṛhaspati he becomes a pupil of Bhārgava, there also he is not satisfied and on the advice of Bhārgava he becomes a disciple of Prahlāda in the guise of a brahmin boy. Like a true disciple Indra serves Prahlāda with great honour and devotion. Then overpleased with his service and sacrifice Prahlāda asks the brahmin ascetic to choose a boon. The brahmin ascetic, that is, Indra in disguise asks Prahlāda to hand him over his *śīla*; this *śīla* was the means by which Prahlāda had acquired lordship over three worlds. Now being asked for this boon Prahlāda became nervous and worried. But there was no other way to escape once the boon had been promised. When Prahlāda was thus seated in worried and excited state of mind, his *śīla* first went out of his body. After *śīla*, *dharma* (embodiment of righteousness) *satya* (truth) *vṛtta* (embodiment of good deeds) and *vala* (strength) went out of the body of Prahlāda one after the other. Lastly went out Śrī of lustrous appearance (*Prabhāmayī devī*). On being asked by Prahlāda about the brahmin-ascetic, Śrī says to Prahlāda. 'O knower of piety, all worlds were under your subjugation because of your *śīla.* So Indra had acquired that *śīla* from you now[13].

This last narrative shows how in course of time the redactors of the *Mahābhārata* had brought a complete change in the character of Prahlāda. Prahlāda though remaining as the lord of demons had acquired all the nicest qualities. He had become an ideal hero, an embodiment of *śīla, dharma, satya, vṛtta, vala* and *Śrī*.

After loss of lordship over the three worlds Prahlāda passes his time in complete detachment. He takes praise and censure equally. He never becomes angry with things that displeases him, and never rejoices at the accession of objects that are agreeable. For him a lump of gold and a clump of earth have equal value. He is steadily engaged in acquiring knowledge leading to liberation. Born of respectable parentage he is possessed of great learning.[14] In emphasising the importance of wisdom (*prajñā*), along with Bali, Namuci and Maṅki, Bhīṣma cites the case of Prahlāda, who after the loss of his earthly prosperity, got the highest felicity through wisdom.[15]

Prahlāda the lord of demons who took pleasure in violating the rules of virtue and piety and who had immeasurable strength befitting a great demon is pictured in the above narratives as a saintly man. He is free from pride, he is born in a noble family; and all his sins have been washed off. He gives discourses on virtue and piety. How to account for this change in the character of Prahlāda? It is well-known fact that *Mahābhārata* is not the work of one hand. Many interpolations have been interwoven into the story by skilful redactors and compilers. Demoniac nature of Prahlāda actually fits in with the tradition of Vedic literature which refers to his fight and enemity with gods. Later redactors are responsible for bringing over a change in his character. Out of the three episodes narrated above the dialogue between Bali and Prahlāda, quoted by Draupadī is found in the didactic sections of Book III; the episode of Indra's discipleship under Prahlāda is found in Book XII (*Śānti parvan*), which has nothing to do with the actual epic, hence Hopkins designates this book as 'pseudoepic'[16]. Again the story of Prahlāda arbitrating a dispute and giving his judgement in favour of the brahmin and against his own son is nothing but brahmanical poetry showing a much later phase of development.

Thus through later additions and inter-polations Prahlāda became an ideal figure, more resembling *parama-haṁsa,*[17] the highest order of sannyāsins.

Prahlāda as *Vibhūti* of Viṣṇu

In tenth Chapter of *Bhagavad-Gītā* Lord Śrīkṛṣṇa describes to Arjuna his divine forms (*ātma-vibhūtayaḥ*) and then says, "Whatever being there is endowed with glory and grace and vigour, know that to have sprung from a fragment of my splendour". In an elaborate narration of the very best of every species, comes Prahlāda. Of lights I am the sun, of stars the moon, of Vedas the *Sāma-Veda*, of gods Indra, of demons Prahlāda (*Prahlāda cāsmi daityānām*)' and so forth. It is quite possible that Prahlāda was thought of as born from a fragment of Lord's splendour (*tejoṁśa sambhavam*), and put on an equal footing with the sacred syllable Om, only after the redactors of the *Mahābhārata* had brought on a change in the demoniac character of Prahlāda.

Once Prahlāda was represented as the fragment of the splendour of Viṣṇu (*tejomśa sambhavam*) not in any myth of the Vedic literature but in the *Bhagavad-Gītā*, the chief devotional book of the Vaisnavites, it is quite natural for Vaisnavite redactors to insert him in the myth of Hiraṇyakaśipu in all types of ordeals only to prove the worth of his devotion of Viṣṇu.

In *Taittirīya Brāhmaṇa* (1.5.10.7) also Prahlāda is referred to as *Kayādhava*.

References

1. In the Vedic literature the practice of adding a matronymic to a person's name is found. Like Prahlāda Kayādhava (of Kayādhu) the other example is Mahidāsa Aitareya (son of Itara, *Chāndogya Upaniṣad* III.16.7). This practice of mentioning a man by reference to his mother's name continued till later times. (Prof. Kane–*History of Dharmaśāstras*, Vol. II, Part-I, p. 194).
2. All references in the *Mahābhārata* are to the Critical Edition.
3. *Das Purāṇa Pañcalakṣaṇa*. Versuch enir Text-geschichte by W. Kirfel, 1927 Bonn.
4. With the change in the character of Prahlāda as a devotee of Viṣṇu later redactors of *Purāṇas* used other epithets for Prahlāda like *dharmavān, ativaiṣṇava*.
5. *Daityānām atha rājānaṁ*
   prahlādṁ ditinandanaṁ
6. *ete cānye ca bahavaḥ sagaṇāḥ daityadānavāḥ/*
   dharmasetum atikramya remire adharmaniścayāḥ//
7. *rathenānena maghavā jitavān śambaraṁ yudhi/*
   namuci-bala-vṛtrau ca prahlāda narakau api//
8. *prahlādam ca nihatyājau tato devādhipo'bhavam./*
   Mahābhārata 12.99.49.
9. *divaḥ prahlādam avasānam ānayam ko me*
   sukhāya prahareta martyaḥ *Mahābhārata*, 14, 9, 30
10. As examples of boundless exaggeration WINTERNITZ (*History of Indian Literature*. Vol. I, Part-II, p. 465, University of Calcutta,

1963) refers to the story of Pururavā and Urvasī. In the *Ṛgveda* Urvasī lived with Pururavas for four years, in *Viṣṇupurāṇa* the two lovers spend 61,000 years in pleasure and delight. When the other Purāṇas speak only of seven hells, the *Bhāgavata* speaks of hundreds and thousands of hells.

11. *atha devāsurayuddham abhūt varṣaśatatrayam/ prahlādaśakrayor bhīmam na kaścid vijayī tayoḥ.//*
Kirfel, p. 406, 37-38.

12. *prahlāda nirjito yuddhe indreṇāmṛtamanthane.* Kirfel, p. 490.78

13. The glorification of Prahlāda has gone so far that *Matsya Purāṇa* (274. 11-12) speaks of Prahlāda as having performed *Mahādāna.*

14. *asaktam dhūtapāpmānaṁ kule jātam bahuśrutam*
Mahābhārata, 12.215.4.

Prahlāda was unattached to all worldly objects. His sins had been washed away. This epithet DHUTAPĀPMA shows that the redactor of the *Mahābhārata* had in his mind the part demonic character of Prahlāda. Of respectable parentage he was possessed of great learning. Without making any change in the family line the redactors ascribe to him birth in a high family.

15. *prajñayā prāpitārtho hi baliraiśvarya saṁkṣaye/ prahlādo namucir-mankistasyāḥ kim vidyate param* MBH. 12. 173.3.

16. Referred to by WINTERNITZ (*History of Indian Literature,* Vol. I, Part II, Calcutta University, 1963), p. 371, Foot-Notes.

17. Of the four types of ascetics-*kuṭicaka, bahūdaka, haṁsa* and *paramahaṁsa* each latter one is superior to each preceding one. Among other virtues *paramahaṁsa,* the ascetic is to stay in an uninhabited house (*śūnyāgāre*) He treats all alike, to him a clod of earth or gold is the same, (*Sarvasamāḥ sarvātmānaḥ samaloṣṭakāñ-canāḥ-Vaikhānasa Smārta-Sūtra*–VIII.9).

CHAPTER 9

A Study of the Man-Lion Myth in the Epics and Purāṇa-Texts

Of the different *avatāras* of Viṣṇu, the only one which is founded on a myth originally proper to Viṣṇu is the Dwarf-incarnation. The three celebrated strides of the Dwarf are rooted in the three steps of the Vedic sun-god Viṣṇu. Similarly the story of the Fish-incarnation is based upon the story of Manu, and the way he was saved from the flood by a great horned-fish as narrated in the *Śatapatha Brāhmaṇa* 1.8.1. 1ff. But unlike these the man-lion myth belongs to the age of epic poetry, though some traditional scholars trace the myth in the *Ṛgveda*.[1] In course of time this Man-lion incarnation of Viṣṇu became so important that a particular Purāṇa like the *Nṛsiṁha Purāṇa,* a quite extensive *Upaniṣad* like the *Nṛsiṁhatāpini,* and a *Pāñcarātra* text like the *Nṛsiṁha Saṁhitā* were composed in honour of this Man-lion incarnation. The Nṛsiṁha sect, which worshipped the Man-lion incarnation of Viṣṇu, must have been quite well-known and widespread.

The first trace of the myth is found in the *Mahābhārata*[2]. In mentioning the important and specific incarnations of God Nārāyaṇa-Viṣṇu, the *Āraṇyaka Parvan*[3] says how the great Lord Puruṣottama having assumed the form of the man-lion killed Hiraṇyakaśipu, who was a great demon of great prowess (*ādidaitya, mahāvīrya*). The other references are found in the Nārāyaṇīya section of the *Mahābhārata.*[4] In these later references the reason for killing Hiraṇyakaśipu is given though briefly. "I shall kill Hiraṇyakaśipu, son of Diti, because he destroys sacrifice, which is for the benefit of god"[5]. "By assuming the form of the boar, the man-lion or the dwarf etc. I shall kill the arrogant enemies of the gods".

Here in a very simple way without exaggeration and hyperbolic description there is reference to the death of Hiraṇyakaśipu, because he was debarring the gods from enjoying the sacrifice.

Then we come to the version of the *Brahmāṇḍa Purāṇa* and the *Vāyu Purāṇa,* both of which texts are rooted in one text-kernel. Pargiter[6] in his *Indian Historical Tradition,* and following him Prof. Kirfel[7], have come to this conclusion. The story of the Man-lion as narrated in the *Vāyu Purāṇa*[8] seems to be nearer to the text-kernel. The exact translation of the myth as put in this Purāṇa is given below :

Hiranyakaśipu practises penance without food, and with his head bent down for hundred thousand years. Then Brahman comes to him, and is pleased to offer him boons. Hiranyakaśipu wants that he should not be killed by any being; dānava-s, asura-s and deva-s should be put on equal footing; and he should be in possession of the supreme lordship of Māruti. Brahman grants him these boons and vanishes. Then Hiranyakaśipu attains the position of an omnipotent divinity by defeating the gods. To whichever quarter he goes, gods along with sages bend down before him. This Hiranyakaśipu of such a great prowess was torn asunder by Viṣṇu in his man-lion form by his nails which are neither wet nor dry[9].

The text as given here does not elucidate the conditions under which he should not die; but at the same time it says that the demon was torn off by the nails which are neither wet nor dry; so it is quite likely that the conditions under which he cannot die were known to the masses. From the loconic manner in which different elements of the story are put here, and from the absence of logical sequence we can infer that this is the earliest version of the story after the *Mahābhārata*. It is possible that by the time of redaction of this text the Man-lion myth was just in a floating state. Some elements of the story which are later greatly developed and elaborated are just hinted here that Hiranyakaśipu should not meet death from any being, and that the gods and the sages were afraid of him.

Though the *Brahmāṇḍa* and the *Vāyu* are based on one text-kernel, one manuscript, yet two different redactors have worked upon the same manuscript; and there has come to existence two different Purāṇas. The redactor of the *Brahmāṇḍa Purāṇa*, unlike the redactor of the *Vāyu*, has improved upon the version of the story as preserved in the text-kernel; there is no doubt about it that redactors of both the *Brahmāṇḍa* and the *Vāyu,* have based their versions on one manuscript. The version of Man-lion myth in the *Brahmāṇḍa Purāṇa* has many textual parallels with the version of the *Vāyu Purāṇa;* yet the Man-lion myth found in the *Brahmāṇḍa Purāṇa*[10] is a version with improved readings. The edition of the *Brahmāṇḍa* has tried to put the missing links of the *Vāyu* in proper place. He has given a sense and unity to the myth by adding or revising the text-kernel as is perhaps found in the *Vāyu.*

In the revised version of the *Brahmāṇḍa Purāṇa* the boons are different in some respects. Instead of the boon in the *Vāyu* that "dānava-s asura-s and deva-s should be put on equal footing", which makes no sense, in the *Brahmāṇḍa* Hiraṇyakaśipu demands that all dānava-s, asura-s and deva-s should be under his control and lordship. As to the boon of the *Vāya* that he should not be killed by any being, clear-cut conditions are added : he should be killed neither by a wet thing nor by a dry thing; he should be killed neither in day nor in night. Brahman grants this boon to him though admitting that the boon is of great significance.[11]

While the *Vāyu* just speaks in one verse (Ch. 67.65) how Hiraṇyakaśipu oppressed the gods, the *Brahmāṇḍa* in six verses (2. 5. 20-25) says that he assumed the form of the moon, the sun and the wind; he became the priest and also the sacrificer: he became the expounder of *mantras,* demons along with gods partook of the Soma juice. On the whole the story of oppression is put in greater detail in the *Brahmāṇḍa.* The method of killing is the same both in *Vāyu* and in the *Brahmāṇḍa.*

Then we come to the *Brahma Purāṇa* version[12]. This version corresponds exactly to the story given in the *Harivaṁśa,*[13] where the simple references of the *Brahmāṇḍa-Vāyu* are given a new shape. The past history of Hiraṇyakaśipu, and the reason why he was killed are given in detail. Hiraṇyakaśipu had practised penance for eleven thousand and five hundred years. Brahman, pleased with his peanance, comes to him encircled by gods, Yakṣas and Kinnaras etc., and tells him to pray for a boon, because he is a great devotee of Brahman. Hiraṇyakaśipu puts up conditions under which he should not die : (*i*) he may not be killed by gods, demons, men or goblins; (*ii*) the curse of enraged sages must not have any effect on him; (*iii*) weapons, mountains, trees, anything wet or dry may not be the cause of his destruction[14]; (*iv*) he can assume the form of any of the gods like Varuṇa, Indra, Yama, Kuvera; (*v*) he can assume the form of any natural element like sun, moon; wind, fire, water or ether. Brahman grants all these boons; but gods are afraid to hear of this. They approach him in fear; but Brahman tells them that the demon must have to reap the fruits of his penance; Viṣṇu would kill him only after he has enjoyed the fruits of his hard penance.

Hiraṇyakaśipu after having obtained the boon, oppressed the gods and the sages. Along with the demons he occupied the heaven; sacrifice meant for god was enjoyed by demons.

The gods appealed to Viṣṇu, who having assured them came to the court of Hiraṇyakaśipu. And there assuming the form of half-man and a half-lion and touching one hand with another (*pāṇiṁ saṁspṛśya pāṇinā*) killed Hiraṇykaśipu along with all other demons with one stroke of his hand (*hatavān ekapāṇinā*). But in all later recensions of the myth Hiraṇyakaśipu has been torn off by the nails of the Man-lion.

The version which we get in the *Viṣṇudharmottara Purāṇa*[15] deviates a little from the account given in the *Brahma Purāṇa* and the *Harivaṁśa* referred to above. Here the Man-lion puts Hiraṇyakaśipu in his lap, and playfully tears him to pieces.

In all the above versions of the myth Prahlāda does not appear at all. Hiraṇyakaśipu is killed because he oppresses the gods and the sages, and because sacrifice of gods is enjoyed by the demons.

Next we come to the *Padma Purāṇa* version[16] of the story. The story as presented here denotes a later phase of development of the legend. There is gorgeous description of the assembly hall of Hiraṇyakaśipu. Bali, Naraka, Vālin, Rāvaṇa, Prahlāda, and so many other demons of great prowess are attending upon Hiraṇyakaśipu. Viṣṇu having assumed the form of Man-lion appears there. Of all the demons present in the assembly Prahlāda is the first to recognise the Man-lion; and he sees the whole universe in him. There are ten verses (5.42.87–96) which depict Prahlāda's vision of the whole universe reflected in the body of the Man-lion[17].

Just in the model of the *Viśva-rūpa-daśrana* of the *Bhagavad-Gītā* Prahlāda describes to his father how he sees the whole universe of oceans, mountains, gods and demons in the body of the Man-lion. Also the whole assembly of demons including Hiraṇyakaśipu and his own self could be seen by Prahlāda in the body of the Man-lion. But though Prahlāda at the sight of this unusual divine form expresses his apprehension, his father Hiraṇyakaśipu does not care; and he orders all the demons to attack the Man-lion. Then it gives an opportunity to the redactor of the Purāṇa to describe the battle between the Man-lion and Hiraṇyakaśipu in verses beginning from 99 to 185. And at last Hiraṇyakaśipu is killed by the Man-lion by his sharp claws.

The only innovation in the *Padma Purāṇa* version is that the redactor makes Prahlāda see the universe in the Man-lion; but his father does not pay any heed to the utterances of Prahlāda, but rather orders *mṛgendro gṛhyatāmeṣaḥ* (*Padma Purāṇa* 5.42.98) "Catch hold of this man-lion." For the first time Prahlāda makes his appearance here though just on the periphery of the incident.

Now what may be the possible cause for inserting Prahlāda here? In the Purāṇas, the genealogy (*Vaṁśānucarita*) is an important subject, where Prahlāda is presented as the eldest son of Hiraṇyakaśipu. This relation must have been quite well-known by this time. Further though in the *Mahābhārata* and in some Vedic texts Prahlāda was pictured as a great demon going against the rules of piety and virtue, gradually the redactors of the *Mahābhārata* had brought a complete change in the character of Prahlāda. He had turned out to be an ideal hero sticking to truth, virtue and piety. And lastly because of this complete change in the character of Prahlāda, the *Bhagavad-Gītā* in chapter X presented Prahlāda as sprung from a fragment of Lord's splendour. In the *Vibhūti-yoga* the Lord says, *Prahlādaś cāśmi daityānām*, "Of the demons I am Prahlāda". Prahlāda's stature went up significantly, once he was mentioned along with Viṣṇu. And moreover this relation of Prahlāda with Viṣṇu (*mama tejo' ṁśa–sambhavaḥ*) was put forth in the *Bhagavad-Gītā*, the holy text of the Vaiṣṇava faith. It is probable, this mention of Prahlāda in the *Bhagavad-Gītā* is the most impelling force, which must have made the redactor of the *Padma Purāṇa* version, put Prahlāda in the assembly of Hiraṇyakaśipu, and made him recognise the universal form in the Man-lion just in the manner of Arjuna seeing the universe in Lord Srī Kṛṣṇa.

But though Prahlāda of all the demons present in the assembly of Hiraṇayakaśipu recognises the divine nature of the Man-lion, he does not recognise the Man-lion to be the incarnation of Viṣṇu. Prahlāda says, *avyaktaṁ paramaṁ divyam kim idaṁ rūpam āgatam* (5.42.88). He is just surprised and puzzled. The question of his great devotion to Viṣṇu does not find any place in this version.

In the *Matsya Purāṇā*[18] the Man-lion myth has been described in three chapters (161–163). The redactor of the *Matsya Purāṇa* has added some new verses for describing the battle between Hiraṇyakaśipu and the Man-lion. Besides, the assembly hall of Hiraṇyakaśipu is depicted as endowed with more pomp and splendour. But the only significant difference of the *Matsya Purāṇa* version of the myth from the *Padma Purāṇa* version is this. In the *Padma* (5.42.85) Prahlāda with his divine form had the vision of the Man-lion (*divyena vapuṣā siṁham apaśyad devam agatam*). In the *Matsya Purāṇa* version (162.2) Prahlāda endowed with divine vision sees the Man-lion (*divyena cakṣuṣā siṁham apaśyad devam agatam*). Of the two readings in the *Padma* and the *Matsya*, '*divyena cakṣuṣā*' is definitely a better reading.

In the eleventh chapter of the *Bhagavad-Gītā* Śrīkṛṣṇa before revealing his universal form speaks to Arjuna, "O Arjuna, you cannot behold me with your human eye. I will bestow on thee the supernatural eye. Behold my divine form" (11.8). Following the line of the Gītā the redactor of the *Matsya Purāṇa* endows Prahlāda with *divya cakṣus,* the angelic eye; and like Arjuna, Prahlāda gets a view of the whole universe in the Man-lion.

Then we come to the version of the Man-lion myth in the *Harivaṁśa.*[19] Here the redactor has followed the *Matsya Purāṇa* version of the story; but some new elements have been added to it.

First of all when Brahman has come to grant boons to Hiraṇyakaśipu, some new conditions have been put forward. Besides the conditions put forward in earlier versions of the story, the new additions are : "Let me not be killed either in the heaven or in the nether region or on this earth or on the etheral region. Let me not die either in day or in night." (41.15).

Then when Hiraṇyakaśipu has begun torturing the gods, all of them go to Viṣṇu. Viṣṇu assures them that he would kill Hiraṇyakaśipu; but when so many conditions have been granted to him by Brahman, and that he might not be killed on these conditions, Viṣṇu is worried as to how Hiraṇyakaśipu is to be killed. He goes to Himālayas to think of the way Hiraṇyakaśipu is to be killed.[20]

As in the earlier versions here also at the appearance of the Man-lion in the assembly of Hiraṇyakaśipu, Prahlāda, afraid of the unusual divine form (*avyakta-prabhavaṁ divyaṁ kim idaṁ rupam adbhutam* 48.8), describes to his father the whole universe reflected in the body of the Man-lion. But his father without caring for the words of Prahlāda orders for a fight. But here Prahlāda just does not desist after pointing out to his father the terrible Man-lion. He with his head bent down meditates upon that terrible form in whom he sees the whole universe reflected (*dadhyan... mahāmatiḥ kiṁcit adhomukhaḥ prāk* 43.17). Unlike earlier versions where Prahlāda is called *vīryavān,* here he is very wise (*mahāmati*).

Another innovation introduced is the conversation of Hiraṇyakaśipu with Śukrācārya, the preceptor of the demons. When the fight between Hiraṇyakaśipou and the Man-lion is in the progress, all sorts of evil portents appear. This is common to the *Padma Purāṇa* version and the *Matsya Purāṇa* version of the story. But Here Hiraṇyakaśipou is curious to know the cause of evil portents from Śukrācārya, who tells him that either the kingdom would be lost, or the king would be killed. But this warning does not have any effect on the demon, who fights with more zeal; and vigour; and in the end he is killed by the sharp long nails of the Man-lion.

Two different versions of the Man-lion myth in the same book *Harivaṁśa* (one in the *Harivaṁśa parvan,* and the other in the *Bhaviṣya parvan*) bring home to us the definite fact that redactors were always busy in making additions and alterations for giving a new shape to each and every Purāṇa.[21] It is difficult to assign any exact date to these Purāṇas. The Man-lion myth in *Harivaṁśa parvāṇa* confined to only thirty-nine verses has been expanded to two hundred and eighty-eight verses spread over six chapters in the *Bhaviṣya parvan.* Description of abnormal splendour of the court of Hiraṇyakaśipu, long tedious description of the quite unnatural and horrible fight between the demon and the Man-lion, exuberance of evil portents and horrible signs seen in the kingdom of the demon–all these dry and irrelevant growths have increased the bulk of the myth in the *Bhaviṣya parvan* of the *Harivaṁśa*.

Except the versions of the *Brahma Purāṇa* and the *Harivaṁśa* (*Harivaṁśa Parvan*) where Hiraṇyakaśipu is killed with the stroke of the hand of the Man-lion, all the other versions show how succeeding redators have developed the myth by expounding particular portions of the myth which appeared to them to be more significant. Almost all verses, all words and all concepts of the younger texts are found in older texts.

One common feature of all these versions is that the Man-lion while going to kill Hiraṇyakaśipu touches one hand with another[22]. The second thing is that when Viṣṇu in the form of the Man-lion kills the demon, the syllable 'Om' always comes to his help[23]. Further after having assumed the man-lion form, Viṣṇu enters the assembly hall of Hiraṇyakaśipu, and kills him there. After Hiraṇyakaśipu is killed, Viṣṇu puts off his man-lion form, and goes back to the northern shore of the milky-ocean[24]. In all these versions, after Brahman has granted boons to Hiraṇyakaśipu, gods apprehending danger from the demon come to Brahman for help, who however shows his helplessness; then the gods come to Viṣṇu, who assures them of his help, and promises to kill the demon. Again the reason for killing Hiraṇyakaśipu is based upon the traditional enmity between gods and demons; the sacrifice supposed to be enjoyed by the gods is enjoyed by the demons; and Hiraṇyakaśipu being a demon torments the ascetics and the sages. Lastly it is not clearly said as to why Hiraṇyakaśipu practised austerities.

When we come to the *Viṣṇu Purāṇa*[25], we find that the Man-lion myth has taken a completely different turn. Though here Hiraṇyakaśipu has committed the sin of divesting the gods of their share of sacrifice, his main fault lies in tormenting his son Prahlāda who is a great devotee of Viṣṇu.

In the *Mahābhārata* Prahlāda did not have any part to play in the Man-lion myth; then in the *Padma Purāṇa,* of all the demons present in the assembly of Hiraṇyakaśipu Prahlāda sees the whole universe reflected in the body of the Man-lion. And in the *Bhaviṣya parvan* of the *Harivaṁśa* which contains the latest redaction of the myth, after getting the vision of the whole universe in the body of the Man-lion, Prahlāda meditates on him when he appears in the assembly of Hiraṇyakaśipu. But in the *Viṣṇu Purāṇa* Prahlāda is the main figure; he has become the greatest devotee of Viṣṇu. In earlier descriptions his demoniac origin was effectively contrasted with his good fortune of seeing the universe in the Man-lion, and his meditation on him. But here the contrast is more effective. Prahlāda born in the race of demons is just a child; and this tender age of Prahlāda and his helplessness are put as effective contrast to the torment and oppression of his father Hiraṇyakaśipu. Oppression of the gods and the sages, or the destruction of their sacrifice do not constitute the main fault of Hiraṇyakaśipu. True to his demoniac nature he tortures Prahlāda to the utmost, because he is a devotee of Viṣṇu. And this is the greatest wrong for which he is punished. Of all the Purāṇas the *Viṣṇu Purāṇa* gives an exaggerated account of the oppressions undergone by Prahlāda. Hiraṇyakaśipu cannot tolerate his devotion to Viṣṇu; so he orders the demons to strike him heavily and repeatedly with the weapons. Snakes bite him with their envenomed fangs. The elephants of the quarters trample upon him. There is an attempt to burn him in fire. Cooks supply him with deadly poison in his food. Priests of Hiraṇyakaśipu take recourse to magic incantiations. A female form with fiery flame is produced; she smites Prahlāda with a fiery flame on his chest, but the weapon breaks to pieces. The demons hurl the boy down from the summit of the palace upon the tops of the mountains. Demon Śambara practises subtle magic devices for his destruction. Then Prahlāda is put before the withering wind; that cold, cutting and dry wind penetrates into his body. When all these devices for killing Prahlāda prove to be of no avail, he is thrown into the ocean; but there he floats upon the waters. Therefore the demons put huge rocks upon him for many thousand miles, and bind him with *nāga-pāśa*.

But Prahlāda begins meditation of Viṣṇu inside the ocean. He realises Viṣṇu as identical with his own self. And when he completely identifies himself with Viṣṇu, the *nāga-pāśa-s* twining round his limbs like serpents give way, The ocean is violently shaken. Prahlāda comes forth out of the ocean, and begins to pray Viṣṇu (1.20.9-13). But surprisingly Viṣṇu appears before Prahlāda not in the Man-lion form as in the earlier versions, but clad in yellow robes (*āvirbabhūva bhagavān pītāmbaradharo hariḥ,* 1.20.14). Viṣṇu is pleased with Prahlāda, and grants him three boons. First boon that Prahlāda begs is that he may have unswerving and unflinching devotion to Viṣṇu. The next boon that Prahlāda asks of Viṣṇu is to pardon his father for the sins he has committed in torturing him. The third boon granted by Viṣṇu is that Prahlāda will attain liberation because of his firm devotion and attachment to Viṣṇu.

Then after the granting of these boons Viṣṇu vanishes. Prahlāda goes to his father; and the demon repents of his cruelty to his son, and treats him with kindness. Thus the whole Man-lion myth is given a different turn.

But the author of the *Viṣṇu Purāṇa* did not have the courage to ignore completely the tradition of earlier Purāṇas, where Hiraṇyakaśipu was killed by the Man-lion. So even after Hiraṇyakaśipu has repented for his past sins, and shed tears for torturing his son (1.20.30-31), the author gets the demon killed by Viṣṇu in the form of the Man-lion. This fact of Viṣṇu's appearing as Man-lion, and killing Hiraṇyakaśipu has been put in a very concise form in only half of the verse (1.20.32)[26].

The terrible fight between Hiraṇyakaśipu and the Man-lion which was described in great details in the earlier versions of the story in the *Padma,* the *Matsya,* the *Bhaviṣya parvan* of the *Harivaṁśa,* and other Purāṇas has completely disappeared. A short pithy sentence (first half of 1.20.32) referring to the killing of Hiraṇyakaśipu by the Man-lion, and Hiraṇyakaśipu's unusual atrocities towards the gods (1.17.2-9) after the grant of boon to him are the only traces left of original Man-lion myth.

The way the Man-lion myth is narrated in the *Viṣṇu Purāṇa* shows that for the author of this Purāṇa *avataravāda* is superfluous. The belief in the incarnation theory as propounded in the *Bhag. Gītā* (4.7), "Whenever there is a decline of righteousness and rise of unrighteousness, O Arjuna, then I incarnate myself" does not have any significance for the author of the *Viṣṇu Purāṇa.* This is the reason for which Hiraṇyakaśipu is not killed. Whenever Prahlāda has been tortured by his father, we find that as a true devotee of Viṣṇu he does not have any ill feeling for his father, The author of the *Viṣṇu Purāṇa* has pictured Prahlāda as a true devotee of Viṣṇu. And as such he sees Viṣṇu in all creatures. When Prahlāda teaches his classmates about the devotion of Viṣṇu, he says, "The whole world is a manifestation of Viṣṇu. Search for the identity in all creatures. True worship of Viṣṇu consists in treating all as identical"[27]. This philosophy is the basis of Prahlāda's love and affection to all those who tried to slay him[28]. So the author of the *Viṣṇu Purāṇa* has given a turn to the conduct of Viṣṇu so that it stands in harmony with the conduct of Prahlāda. Killing of Hiraṇyakaśipu would not have been nice in the context when points like devotion to Viṣṇu and grace of Viṣṇu are the main themes with our author.

Parāśara in introducing Prahlāda speaks of him as one who had the highest devotion to Viṣṇu (*paramāṁ bhaktiṁ ya uvāha janārdane,* 1.15.144). For showing this power of *bhakti* Prahlāda has been pictured as a child. And though a child Prahlāda has withstood all the torments heaped upon him. He has achieved the final victory, he has come out safe and sound from the ocean, where he was thrown bound by *nāgapāśas.* Thus the victory of the child is the victory of *bhakti.* This miraculous element in the character of Prahlāda comes out not only when he escapes unhurt from the different ordeals, but when he even as a child gives sermons on Vaiṣṇavism to his classmates. Referring to this Prof. Otto says :[29] "By the time the *Viṣṇu Purāṇa* was written, Vaiṣṇavism had been a strong missionary religion. It had a long fight not only against Buddhism but also against other sects and beliefs. Prahlāda in the *Viṣṇu Purāṇa* acts as a missionary. He gathers his classmates around him, and gives them lessions on Viṣṇu."

Then we take up the myth as narrated in the *Bhāgavata Purāṇa.*[30] Hiraṇyakaśipu's brother Hiraṇyākṣa was slain by Viṣṇu in his Boar incarnation. So Hiraṇyakaśipu is greatly agitated with wrath and grief. In his anger and fury against Viṣṇu he orders the demons to kill the sacrificers, and upset the religious order (7.2.21-26; 39-49). In order to make himself invincible and immortal, he practises penance in a valley of Mandara mountain. With his arms uplifted, and his eyes turned towards the sky he remains standing on the tips of his toes. He continues *tapas* for one hundred divine years. Finally the demon is covered with ant-hills, grass and reeds, while his skin, flesh, marrow and blood are simultaneously eaten up by a large number of white-ants (7.3.1-38; 7.4.1-3).

Thus the author of the *Bhāgavata* has supplied the reason for the *tapas* practised by Hiraṇyakaśipu. And the myth of Hiraṇyakaśipu and his death by the Man-lion have been connected with the immediately preceding *avatāra* of Viṣṇu. In the earlier versions of the myth in the *Brahma Purāṇa,* the *Padma Purāṇa* and the *Harivaṁśa,* there was the story of Hiraṇyakaśipu's penance; the *Viṣṇu Purāṇa* mentioned it very briefly. But the author of the *Bhāgavata* has again taken up the story of Hiraṇyakaśipu's penance, and has given a detailed description of it.

When Hiraṇyakaśipu is engaged in religious austerities, a smoky fire comes out of his head. That fire after having spread in all directions begins to scorch the higher, the middle and the lower regions. The rivers, the oceans and the earth with the islands and the mountains are greatly agitated. The planets with the stars fall down from their respective places. The ten quarters and the heavens are scorched with the fire coming out of the head of Hiraṇyakaśipu. The gods are no longer able to reside in heaven; they are afraid that all the regions will be destroyed (7.3.3-6). Gods praying for help come to Brahman, and tell him that the demon wants to take his position, and that he is determined to upset the laws of the universe (7.3.6-13).

Then Brahman goes to the demon, tells him that he is pleased with his marvellous penance, and that he is ready to grant him boons. Brahman then sprinkles holy water from his *kamaṇḍalu* on the body of Hiraṇyakaśipu eaten up by white ants. Then like fire coming out of fuel Hiraṇyakaśipu comes out of the reeds and anthills, refreshed and youthful with energy and vigour (7.3.14, 16-23).

Hiraṇyakaśipu speaks out his wish : "Let not my death result from any being of Thy creation. Let me not die in-doors or out-of-doors, during night or day, by means of weapons, on earth or in the skies. Let me not be killed by men or animals, by animate or inanimate beings, demons or great reptiles. Grant me matachless might in battle, undisputed lordship over corporeal beings, the glory of all the guardians of the world, and everything that Thou possessest. And let me have all those luxuries as are enjoyed by persons having power of asceticism (7.3.35–38)." Brahman confers all these boons on Hiraṇyakaśipu, and goes back to his place.

Here as we see, the demon by the force of the magical power of his *tapas* has got whatever he wanted. He has secured all the advantages of which gods are afraid. And the number of conditions with which he has tried to protect himself has become so complex that only the Man-lioṇ can kill him.

After getting the desired boons Hiraṇyakaśipu acts up to his hostile feelings against Viṣṇu. He rules in heaven in place of Indra. All the divinities except Brahman, Viṣṇu and Maheśvara pay their obeisance to him. He carries on a tyrannical rule over all beings.

Now the gods take refuge in Viṣṇu, and offer their prayers to Him (7.4.22-23). After a few days, a voice resembling the rumbling of clouds and filling all the quarters, coming out from some unseen source is heard by the gods. The voice speaks out: "I know all about the oppression of the demon. I will mete out fit punishment to him. You all wait till the proper time. I will slay him, when he will persecute his own son, the high-souled Prahlāda." (7.4.24-28).

In the *Harivaṁśa* (*Bhaviṣya parvan*) Viṣṇu was personally present before the gods to assure them that he would kill Hiraṇya-kaśipu. But here in the *Bhāgavata* when the gods pray to Viṣṇu, He remains invisible, even though He makes his voice heard. Thus Viṣṇu has become super-eminent. His position has gone up higher in the imagination of his devotees. He has become the absolute monarch over the gods; and the gods only pray to Him, but cannot see Him.

In the earliest mention of the myth in the *Mahābhārata* (12.326.73) Viṣṇu kills Hiraṇyakaśipu because he destroys the sacrifice (*haniṣyāmi yajñaghnaṁ diti-nandanaṁ*). But now sacrifice has fallen into insignificance. Hiraṇyakaśipu's tyranny over the gods or his destruction of sacrifice is of no importance to Viṣṇu. Since the time of the *Viṣṇu Purāṇa* devotion to Viṣṇu (*Viṣṇu-bhakti*) has attained utmost significance. So Viṣṇu promises to act not because Hiraṇyakaśipu is oppressive, but only when he tortures his son Prahlāda, an ideal devotee of Viṣṇu. So torture of Prahlāda now becomes the immediate cause of Viṣṇu's incarnation. By the time of the *Bhāgavata* the myth of Prahlāda had been quite well-known. The author of the *Bhāgvata* says that Prahlāda's virtues have been sung before by poets again and again (7.4.34).

In chapter fifth of the seventh book of the *Bhāgavata* Hiraṇyakaśipu's encounter with Prahlāda begins. Prahlāda along with children of other demons has been taking lessons with Saṇḍa and Amarka, the two sons of Sukrācārya. Hiraṇyakaśipu once places Prahlāda on his lap, and asks him as to the lesson he has learnt. In reply thereto Prahlāda says that people, whose intellect is confused by false conceptions of ego and egoism, should go to the forest, and meditate on Hari. At this Hiraṇyakaśipu laughs in derision, and sends back his son to his teachers. The teachers ask him as to wherefrom he has learnt about Viṣṇu. Prahlāda gives a witty reply that like a piece of iron approaching a magnet by itself, his mind is drawn towards Cakrapāṇi. Then the teachers threaten him with a cane, and reproach him; then they instruct him on *trivarga* : *Dharma, Artha* and *Kāma.* And being convinced of Prahlāda's thorough knowledge about different policies like *sāman, dāna, daṇḍa, bheda,* teachers take him to his father, after his mother has anointed him with perfumes, and decorated him with ornaments.

Prahlāda greets his father by falling prostrate at his feet. The demonking blesses him, and embraces him warmly with his two arms. Then he asks him to narrate some of the best lessons he has taken from his teachers. Prahlāda as an ideal devotee of

Viṣṇu gives the pointed reply to his father that devotion to Viṣṇu, which is nine-fold is the best of all teachings; and that devotion consists of : hearing the holy name of Viṣṇu, recitation of holy names, recollection of them, paying service to his lotus-feet, worshipping him, adoring him, serving him, and self-abnegation for the sake of meditation upon him[31].

Hiraṇyakaśipu angrily sends for the teachers, and asks them as to why they have tought him this nonsense. The teachers reply that he is naturally devoted to Viṣṇu. Then the demon asks his son about the source of his knowledge. Prahlāda in three verses (7.5.30–32) tells his father that only worship of Viṣṇu can lead to liberation; and rather in a veiled reference to his teachers, he says that, those persons of vitiated understanding, who accept as teachers the people absorbed in worldly objects, fall into the pit like the blind man led by the blind. At this Hiraṇyakaśipu becomes blind with anger, and throws him off on the ground from his lap, and orders the demons to kill Prahlāda without delay. Remembering the death of his brother Hiraṇyakśa at the hands of Viṣṇu, he says, 'This boy has rather killed my brother' (ayaṁ me bhrātṛhā, 7.5.35), as he is worshipping Viṣṇu, the slayer of his uncle.

As we find here, Hiraṇyakaśipu's character has been painted just like a loving father. He fondles and embraces his son. Unlike the author of the *Viṣṇu Purāṇa* the author of the *Bhāgavata* does not make the demon furious all of a sudden, when he knows about Prahlāda's faith in Viṣṇu. His demonaic nature is revealed only when, in his second meeting with Prahlāda, the latter affirms his devotion to Viṣṇu.

As ordered by Hiraṇyakaśipu the demons attack Prahlāda with tridents; but the strokes of the demons prove unavailing against Prahlāda. Then Hiraṇyakaśipu tries to kill him by means of huge snakes, by employing huge elephants, by use of magic spell, by throwing him down from lofty mountain peaks, by his own illusive powers, by confining him in a solitary cell, by mixing poison with his food, by starving him, by leaving him alone in mountains and by various other means; but he does not succeed.

Each ordeal through which Prahlāda had to pass is described in detail in the *Viṣṇu Purāṇa.* But the author of the *Bhāgavata* gives a short summary of all these ordeals narrated in the *Viṣṇu Purāṇa,* and adds a few of his own. For instance, Prahlāda's confinement in a solitary hall, the attempt to starve him to death, leaving him alone on the mountains–these are the innovations of the author of the *Bhāgavata.* But all main devices of torture have been borrowed from the *Viṣṇu Purāṇa.*

When all the devices for killing Prahlāda have failed, Hiraṇyakaśipu is perplexed. He is afraid of his own death because of the tortures meted out to Prahlāda. Thus the author of the *Bhāgavata* has rather made a psychological study of the character of Hiraṇyakaśipu.

Then Śaṇḍa and Amarka, teachers of Prahlāda, advise Hiraṇyakaśipu that with advance in age Prahlāda's ideas will change. And Hiraṇyakaśipu orders the teachers to instruct Prahlāda on *dharma, artha* and *kāma,* the religious practices of kings who have married and become householders. After teaching for some days teachers leave for their homes for attending to some households duties. Prahlāda makes use of this opportunity, and calls together all his classmates; and he gives them a long discourse on philosophy and devotion to Viṣṇu. This miraculous element in the story of a child like Prahlāda giving lessons to his classmates is given also in the *Viṣṇu Purāṇa* (1.17.54-91). And here Prahlāda is just pictured as a boy residing in the house of his preceptor (*papāṭha bālapāṭhyāni gurugehaṁ gato'rbhakaḥ*) (1.17.10). But in the *Viṣṇu Purāṇa* no explanation is given for this miraculous trait in the character of a child (*arbhaka*) like Prahlāda. The *Bhāgavata* (7.5.36) on the other hand speaks Prahlāda as a boy of five years old (*pañcahāyana*). In this Purāṇa it is stated that when Prahlāda gives lessons on Vaiṣṇavism to his class-mates, naturally they are surprised as to how a boy of five is endowed with a such a deep knowledge of Viṣṇu, as he is always confined in his home and has no other teachers except Saṇḍa and Amarka, the two sons of Śukrācārya. Here the author of the *Bhāgavata* creates an occasion for describing the past history of Prahlāda in order to explain his miraculous wisdom and devotion to Viṣṇu.

In answering the question of his classmates Prahlāda narrates the following story (7.7.2-16.). When Hiraṇyakaśipu was practising penance on the Mandara mountain, gods started a war against the demons. Demons fled away to different quarters, but Indra imprisoned the wife of Hiraṇyakaśipu. At that time she was carrying Prahlāda in her womb. Indra wanted to kill the baby just after its birth. However accidentally Nārada came there, and told Indra that the foetus existing in her womb was a very devoted follower of Viṣṇu, a *mahābhāgavata.* Out of respect to the words of the divine sage Indra released her.

Nārada took the wife of Hiraṇyakaśipu to his hermitage. There this chaste pregnant lady served the divine sage with great reverence for securing the well-being of her foetus and for easy delivery. And Nārada gave instructions on the real nature of religion, and instilled true knowledge in the mind of this lady carrying Prahlāda in her womb. The lady because of being a woman and because of the length of the intervening time forgot all those teachings; but because of the great favour shown by Nārada, Prahlāda remembered all these teachings which he heard while in the womb.

Thus by alluding to the past history of Prahlāda the author the *Bhāgavata* has made the traditional account of the Man-lion myth quite logical and systematic. This innovation has certainly given a literary shape to the old myth.

In chapter eighth of the *Bhāgavata* (7th Book) the story reaches its climax. Prahlāda's teaching to his class-mates has quite a dramatic effect; all the children have completely forgotten the lessons imparted to them by their teachers; they have their minds bent towards the single purpose, namely attachment to Lord Viṣṇu. This frightens the teachers who immediately report the matter to Hiraṇyakaśipu.

Now Hiraṇyakaśipu, furious like a serpent trodden upon by the feet (*sarpaḥ pādāhāta iva,* 7.8.5), calls upon his son and rebukes him. He asks his son to tell him the source of his strength. Prahlāda all the while remaining in a submissive posture with his hands folded says, "Oh king, that Supreme God, who is the controller of every thing including Brahman and others, is the source of my strength. And He is also the source of power and strength of yours as well as of others (7.8.8). At this satirical reply of his son the demon-king Hiraṇyakaśipu orders Prahlāda to show him his Lord : "If He is present everywhere, why then is he not existent in the pillar?" (*yadi sa sarvatra, kasmāt stambhe na vidyate* 7.8.13). "I shall now sever thy head because of your useless boasting before me. Let Hari, your sole refuge, come to your protection." (7.8.14).

Repeatedly cursing Prahlāda in the most abusive language Hiraṇyakaśipu jumps down from his throne, and strikes the pillar with his fist. Thus the author of the *Bhāgavata* creates a fitting situation for the appearance of the Man-lion. Hiraṇyakaśipu's attitude and behaviour towards his son are presented in a quite graphic and vigorous style in order to prepare the ground for the appearance of the Man-lion. Just before describing the appearance of the Man-lion, the author of the *Bhāgavata* speaks of Hiraṇya-kaśipu as looking at Prahlāda with vicious and crooked eyes (*īkṣamāṇaḥ pāpena tiraścīnena cakṣuṣā,* 7.8.4.), breathing like a serpent trodden by the feet (*sarpaḥ pādāhata iva śvasan,* 7.8.5), grasping his sword and jumping down from his beautiful throne, and giving a blow to the pillar with his fist (*khaḍgaṁ pragṛhya utpatito varāsanāt stambhaṁ tatāḍātibalaḥ svamuṣṭinā,* 7.8.15).

After all this vaunting and boasting when the demon strikes the pillar with his fist, there is produced a terrific sound inside the pillar. To testify to the words of His devotee, and also to assert His omnipresence, Viṣṇu with his Man-lion form appears in that assembly-hall from the very pillar struck by the demon. The author of the *Bhāgavata* in three verses (7.8.20–22) gives a vivid picture of the terrible and ferocious Man-lion not forgetting to mention his sharp-nails serving the purpose of weapons.

When the Man-lion kills the hosts of demons with his Sudarśana cakra, Hiraṇyakaśipu though sure in his heart that "Hari, the god of the potent energy of illusion has thought out this novel means of bringing about my death" (7.8.23), does not hesitate to give a good fight. The fight between Hiraṇyakaśipu and the Man-lion is depicted in eight verses (7.8.24-31) in Kāvya style. The similes used by the author are not without charm. The demon disappears from sight like an insect fallen into fire (*alakṣito' gnau patitaḥ pataṅgamaḥ*, 7.8.24); the Man-lion catches hold of the demon like Garuḍa seizing a serpent (*mahoragaṁ tārkṣya-suto yathāgrahīt,* 7.8.26); the demon was caught by the Man-lion like a rat seized by a serpent (*vyālo yathā ākhum*, 7.8.29). Finally the Man-lion carries the demon to the threshold of the assembly hall; and there placing him on his thighs tears open his bowels and entrails like Garuḍa tearing a venomous snake to pieces (7.8.29). Then putting on the entrails of the demon as his garland the Man-lion appeared like a lion that had killed an elephant (7.8.30). By this process of killing all the conditions that the demon demanded from Brahman are fulfilled.

The Man-lion myth as depicted in the *Bhāgavata* helps us to make an estimate of the development of Vaiṣṇavism by the time the *Bhāgavata Purāṇa* was redacted. We know that in the *Harivaṁśa* version of the myth (*Bhaviṣya parvan,* 41.40) Viṣṇu goes to the Himalayas to think of the form he has to take for killing the demon. But here in the *Bhāgavata* he even does not go to the assembly-hall of Hiraṇyakaśipu. All of a sudden he appears there from a pillar. And this miraculous appearance of Viṣṇu from a pillar, which has definitely added to the aesthetic beauty of the myth, and which as the most popular part of the myth is known to every one of us, proves that Viṣṇu's omnipresence and omnipotence had been firmly established by this time.

After killing Hiraṇyakaśipu the Man-lion takes his seat on a beautiful throne in that assembly-hall; and because of his dreadful appearance expressive of his great rage and wrath, gods like Brahman and Rudra are unable to approach him. Even

Lakṣmī, on seeing that terrible form is frightened. Then at the request of Brahman, Prahlāda approaches the Man-lion, and prays to him in a hymn of forty-three verses (7.9.8-50), being pacified by which the Man-lion's anger vanishes.

The Man-lion pleased with Prahlāda asks him to choose any boon; but Prahlāda desires none of them, because he was unflinchingly devoted to Viṣṇu with a singleness of purpose (*ekāntitvāt bhagavati naicchat tān asurottamaḥ,* 7.9.55).

The very fact that Prahlāda alone to the exclusion of two members of the trinity like Brahman and Śiva could be able to pacify the Man–lion points to the fact that Prahlāda had attained a super-eminent position as a devotee of *Viṣṇu*; and *bhakti,* emotional surrender to Viṣṇu was regarded as the best way to liberation.

The myth should have come to close here after Prahlāda was reluctant to ask for any boon, but the author of the *Bhāgavata* again adds thirty-four verses in the beginning of Ch. ten. Prahlāda again asks for the boon of complete eradication of desire from his mind (kāmānāṁ hṛdy asaṁroham, 7.10.7). The Man-lion grants him this boon and asks Prahlāda to occupy the throne of his father for one Manvantara only.

Then Prahlāda remembers his father, and as in the *Viṣṇu Purāṇa* here he prays that his father may be purified of all his sins for defying the great divinity and for persecutions meted out to him. In the *Viṣṇu Purāṇa* Hiraṇyakaśipu who is alive, has been cleansed of his sins, and pardoned; but here in the *Bhāgavata* the Man-lion declares that because of the birth of a devotee of Viṣṇu like Prahlāda in his family, Hiraṇyakaśipu along with his last twenty-one generations has been sanctified (*trisaptabhiḥ pitā pūtaḥ pitṛbhiḥ saha te'nagha* 7.10.18).

Afterwards Prahlāda as advised by the Man-lion performs the last rites of his father. Then Brahman who was previously afraid to approach the Man-lion, now comes forward to the Man-lion having a graceful appearance (*prasāda-sumukham,* 7.10.25), and praises him in four verses (7.10.26-29), where he says, "Whoever shall meditate on this auspicious form of thine (the Man-lion form) shall be protected from all dangers, and even from that cruel Death". Thus Brahman's prayer is utilised to emphasise the practical application of the myth in day-to-day life.

But just after Brahman finished his prayer, the Man-lion warns the Four-faced God not to grant any boon to the demons in future, which is like offering milk to serpents (7.10.30). After that the Man-lion disappears. This warning to Brahman only shows that by the time the *Bhāgavata* was written, Brahman had completely fallen into insignificance.

Thus we find that through revision and additions by different redactors the original simple episode of the *Mahābhārata* has assumed such a great significance. In *Agni Purāṇa* which describes the manners and customs of the Hindus of a later period, it is found that this worship of the Man-lion has been very common, specially at the time when the king goes out on an expedition.

References

1. KṚṢNĀCĀRYA in his interpretation of the '*dve virūpe*' sūkta (*Ṛgveda* 1.95) tries to prove the existence of the myth in the *Ṛgveda* (*Kṛṣṇācāryaviracitaṁ dve-virūpe-sūktabhāṣyam,* edited by V.S. Bhide, published by Bhārata Itihāsa Saṁśodhaka Maṇḍaḷa, Poona, 1968).
2. Reference is to the Critical Edition, Poona, 1927-66.
3. *Mbht.* 100.20.
4. *Mbht.* 12.326.72-84; and 12.337.36.
5. *Sura-kārye haniṣyami yajñaghnaṁ ditinandanam Mbht* 12.326.73.
6. P. 23, *Indian Historical Tradition By Pargiter.*
7. Introduction, pp. X-XIII, *Das Purāṇa Pañcalakṣaṇa* by Willibald Kirfel, Bonn, 1927.
8. *Vāyu Purāṇa,* Ānandāśrama Sanskrit Series, 49, Poona, 1905, ch. 67. 61-66.
9. *nakhaistu tena nirbhinnā / nārdraśuṣkā nakhāḥ smṛtāḥ // Vāyu* 67.66
10. *Brahmāṇḍa Purāṇa,* Venkateswar Press, Bombay, 1857, 2.5. 13-29.

11. *mahān ayaṁ varas tāta / vṛto ditisuta tvayā // Brahmāṇḍa,* 2.5.18.
12. *Brahma Purāṇa,* Ānandāśrama Sanskrit Series, 1895, ch. 213. 44-79.
13. *Harivaṁśa*, Chitraśālā Press, Poona, 1936; *Harivaṁśaparvan,* Ch. 41.40-78.
14. According to Prof. Kane some of these elements of the story of the destruction of Hiraṇyakaśipu by Viṣṇu in the Man-lion form are supplied by the story of the slaughter of the demon Namuci by Indra at dawn with the foam of waters, since Indra had agreed with Namuci that "he would not slay him by day or by night, with the dry or the moist, with the palm or with the fist, with staff or bow etc." (*Śatapatha Brāhmaṇa.* 12.7.3.1-4)–*History of Dharmaśāstra,* Poona, Vol. II, pp. 718-719.
15. *Viṣṇu-dharmottara Purāṇa,* Venkateśwara Press, Bombay, 1934, 1.54.
16. *Padma Purāṇa,* Vols. I-IV, Ānandāśrama Edition, Poona, 1893- 1894, 5.42.1-197.
17. *tato dṛṣtvā mahābhāgaṁ kālacakram ivāgatam*
    nāraṣiṁhavapuśchannaṁ bhasmachannam ivānalam
    Hiraṅyakaśipoḥ putraḥ Prahlādo nāma vīryavān
    divyena vapuṣā siṁham apaśyad devam āgatam
    Padma, 5.42.84-85.
18. *Matsya Purāṇa* Ānandāśrama Sanskrit Series, 54, Poona, 1907.
19. *Harivaṁśa,* Chitraṣālā Press, 1936; Bhaviṣyaparvan, Chs. 41-47.
20. *so'cireṇaiva kālena himavatpārśvam āgataḥ /*
    kiṁ tu rūpaṁ sāmāsthāya nihanmyenaṁ mahāsuram //
    Harivaṁśa, Bhavisyaparvan, 41.40.
21. In spite of the fact that both the *Vāyu Purāṇa* and the *Brahmāṇḍa Purāṇa* developed from the same kernel, it is difficult to fix any exact date for the *Vāyu Purāṇa.* Redactors were always busy in making revisions, additions and interpolations to these anonymous texts. So Prof. Kirfel observes: On the basis of Bāṇa's reference to the *Vāyu Purāṇa* in his *Harṣacarita* (Third Ucchhvāsa) as *munigītam ati-pṛthu jagadvyāpi pāvanaṁ tadapi,* we cannot decide whether Bāṇa refers to the text as it is available at present on the common text-kernel of the *Brahmāṇḍa-Vāyu* or to a text completely different from any of the above. (*Das Purāṇa Pañcalakṣaṇa,* Introduction, p. XIX.)
22. *pāṇiṁ saṁspṛśya pāṇinā,*
    Harivaṁśa, Harivaṁśaparvan 41.76. *Brahmapurāṇa,* 213.77.
23. *tatra oṅkārasahāyena vidārya nihato yudhi,*
    Harivaṁśa Bhaviṣyaparvan, 47.14.
    Matsya, 163.94; *Padma* 5.42.186.

24. *kṣīrodasya uttaraṁ kulaṁ jagāma Harīśvaraḥ,*
Padma, 5.42.195; *Matsya,* 163.105;
Harivaṁśa, Bhaviṣyaparvan, 47.35.

25. *Viṣṇupurāṇa,* (Gītā Press, Gorakhpur, Saṁvat 2024) 1st Khaṇḍa, Chs. 16-20.

26. *pitaryuparatiṁ nīte narasiṁhasvarūpiṇā,* 1.20.32.

27. *sarvatra daityās samatām upeta*
samatvam ārādhanam acyutasya, 1st Khaṇḍa, 17.90.

28. *ye hantum āgatā dattaṁ yair viṣam yair hutāśanaḥ /*
yair diggajair ahaṁ kṣuṇṇo daṣṭaḥ sarpaiś ca yair api /
teṣv ahaṁ mitrabhāvena samaḥ pāpo' smi na kvacit /
1st Khaṇḍa, 18.42-43.

29 *Viṣṇu-Nārāyaṇa,* Rudolf OTTO, Jena, 1923, p. 56.

30. *Bhāgavatapurāṇa* (Gītā Press, Gorakhpur, Saṁvat 2022) 7th Book, chs. 1-10.

31. 7th Book, 5.23-24. Here in the nine-fold *bhakti* mentioned by Prahlāda, we see the latest development of the concept of *bhakti* as presented in the *Bhāgavata.*

32. 7th Book, 5.51-52.

CHAPTER 10

Birth of Agastya and Vasiṣṭha

Vasiṣṭha is one of the foremost seers of ancient times. In the *Ṛgveda* he appears as the family priest of Sudāsa and Bharatas. He is regarded as the "the seer" of the entire seventh Maṇḍala of the *Ṛgveda.* It was the sage Vasiṣṭha at whose request Indra made the river Paruṣṇī shallow and easily fordable to enable king Sudāsa to escape to the other bank (*Ṛgveda* VII.18.5). As referred to by Prof. Velankar, (*Ṛgveda Maṇḍala* VII, Introduction p. XXIV) the seers of the Vasiṣṭha family represented the orthodox priests in contrast to the Viśvāmitras, the progressive group of bold reformers. In *Rāmāyaṇa* there is one Vasiṣṭha who is the preceptor of the ruling family of Ayodhyā; (*Rāmāyana* II.5.1). An independent treatise like *Yoga-Vāsiṣṭha* is attributed to Vasiṣṭha. Lastly the most remarkable aspect in the character of Vasiṣṭha is that he is one of the Saptarṣis (group of seven seers).[1] It is clear that in the cultural tradition of our country the Vedic sage Vasiṣṭha and the seers born in his family, the Vasiṣṭhas, occupied a pre-eminent position. The other sage Agastya is no less important. He is the seer of the hymns 165-189 of the first maṇḍala of the *Ṛgveda*. Āryan expansion to the south is reflected in the story of Agastya meeting the Vindhya mountain and responsible for altering its height. The Vindhya-mountain growing in its height obstructed the path of the sun. It is the venerable sage Agastya at whose feet the lordly mountain bends down in humility and makes the southern region easily accessible for the sage (*Mahābhārata*, Āraṇyaka Parvan, 104. 1-115). In the *Rāmāyaṇa* he marries Lopāmudrā, the daughter of the king of Vidarbha (*Rāmāyaṇa* V.24.11). Like Vasiṣṭha, one of the Saptarṣi, the brightest star in the southern hemisphere bears the name of Agastya. The purpose of the present study is to trace the birth of these two venerable sages in the Vedic texts, Epics and the Purāṇas.

Vedic Texts and Ancillaries

***Ṛgveda* VII. 33.9-14 :** No doubt the *Ṛgveda* is a collection of hymns composed by the ancient seers in honour of the different divinities. Though primarily it contains hymns in honour of various divinities of nature, through different myths, legends and anecdotes the *Ṛgveda* refers to the stories of secular nature like the episode of Purūravas and Urvaśī, (X.95) the incest of Yama and Yamī (X.10.1-14) etc. Likewise the hymn no. 33 of the 7th maṇḍala referring to the Dāśarājña war speaks of Vasiṣṭha who played a prominent part in it. In order to glorify the family of the Vasiṣṭhas the *Ṛgvedic* seer almost deifies Vasiṣṭha. The hymn no. 33 is devoted to the description of the circum- stances under which Vasiṣṭha referred to as direct descendant of one of the chief gods of the Vedic Aryans came down to dwell among the Bharatas to help and guide them. The particular mission for which Vasiṣṭha comes down to this world of mortals is for fostering worship and sacrifice to the Vedic gods among the Vedic Āryans. And in narrating the circumstances which led to the celestial birth of Vasiṣṭha, it (*Ṛgveda* VII.33.9-14) says : "Mitra and Varuṇa were the presiding deities of a Soma sacrifice. In the sacrifice at the sight of the celestial nymph Urvaśī they became very passionate which resulted in their dropping of the semen. The semen partly fell in an earthern pitcher and partly outside it. The semen falling outside the pitcher was held by the gods in a lotus flower and carried to Urvaśī for disposal and finally Vasiṣṭha was born (9d-10ab). So the *Ṛgvedic* poet calls Vasiṣṭha a son of Mitra and Varuṇa born of Urvaśī, but born from her mind (मनसोऽधिजात:), not from her body. This is the first birth of Vasiṣṭha. From the semen deposited in the pitcher Māna (Agastya) was born. It is Agastya who brought away Vasiṣṭha from the celestial clan to the people *i.e.* the Bharatas. In the *mantra* no. 14 the poet of the hymn calls upon the Bharatas, who wait upon him with devotion as he had chosen to be with them, brought his descendants, always supporting the latter in their priestly work.

In the above account we get two different aspects of the birth of Vasiṣṭha. It is the semen of the twin divinities Mitra and Varuṇa, which is the cause of the birth of Vasiṣṭha. Along with divinities Mitra and Varuṇa, there is Urvaśī. Added to that by the magical power of a celestial hymn (ब्रह्मणा दैव्येन) the Viśvedevāḥ held the semen of both the divinities in a lotus. Thus Vasiṣṭha's divine birth has been kept unsullied : Mitra and Varuṇa, the twin divinities famous in *Ṛgveda,* Urvaśī, the divine nymph, Visvedevāḥ the protector of the semen, the divine *mantra* chanted for its protection. The poet speaks of Vasiṣṭha's second birth as a human sage though not in detail. It merely says that Agastya took him to the people (Bharatas) who were greatly benefited by the efficacy of his priestly services. Incidentally the hymn refers to the birth of Māna from the semen deposited in the pitcher. On a comparison of the birth of Vasiṣṭha and Agastya one can notice that Vasiṣṭha has been represented both as divine and earthly (Agastya introduces him to the human society) *i.e.* he is a semi-divine sage. But in case of Agastya his divine birth (कुम्भे रेतः सिषिचतुः समानम्, ततो ह मान उदियाय मध्यात्) has been referred to and his birth as a human sage has been completely neglected.

Atharvaveda : In *Atharvaveda* (IV.29.3) Mitra and Varuṇa– the dual divinities show their special favour to Agastya and Vasiṣṭha along with other sages like Atri, Aṅgiras and Jamadagni. The seer of this hymn is Vasiṣṭha and the hymn deals with praise and prayer to Mitra and Varuṇa.

Nirukta : Yāska, (6th cent. B.C.) while expounding the meaning of the word Uravaśī quotes the eleventh *mantra* of the 33rd Sūkta of the 7th maṇḍala. In his comment (V. 13) on the said *mantra* he repeats the myth as related in the *Ṛgveda*. At the sight of Urvaśī, the seminal fluid of Mitra and Varuṇa falls down, and Vasiṣṭha is born from that seminal fluid held by Viśvedevāḥ in a *puṣkara*[2] (the atmosphere). Thus Vasiṣṭha is spoken of as born from the mind of Urvaśī.

Bṛhaddevatā : The *Bṛhaddevatā* (4th cent. B.C.) is the oldest systematic collection of legends. Through Aditi, one of the daughters of Dakṣa, Kaśyapa had twelve sons (dvādaśādityāḥ). The *Bṛhaddevatā* just refers to the names of these twelve Ādityas, but with respect to Mitra and Varuṇa the text (V.143-155) in *Ṛgvedic* tradition develops the story leading to the birth of Agastya and Vasiṣṭha. At the sight of the nymph Urvaśī at a sacrifical session the semen of Mitra and Varuṇa was effused and fell into a jar.[3] Both the ascetics Agastya and Vasiṣṭha were born. Vasiṣṭha was found standing on a lotus supported by Viśvedevāḥ.

The *Ṛgveda* (VII.33.10) referred to the two births of Vasiṣṭha; the semen of Mitra and Varuṇa and its final disposal by Urvaśī, the first birth, Agastya taking him to the people, the Bharatas, the second birth. Unlike *Ṛgveda* the *Bṛhaddevatā* does not speak of Agastya introducing Vasiṣṭha to the human society. But with the sole purpose of emphasizing the glory and importance of Vasiṣṭha as a divine sage the text adds an interesting anecdote to Vasiṣṭha. The *Ṛgvedic* text very often with reference to Vasiṣṭha has given an etymological explanation of the name (II.9.1, VII.1.8, X.15,8, X.95.17) where it is used as an adjective meaning best, excellent (*Vasumattama, Vasayitṛtama*). Śaunaka takes up this thread and says : नामास्य गुणतः जज्ञे वसतेः श्रैष्ठ्यकर्मणः– 156a the name Vasiṣṭha is derived from the root " *Vas*" meaning pre-eminence. And in order to justify this pre-eminent nature of Vasiṣṭha Śaunaka introduces a new story, (*Bṛhaddevatā*-V.156-159); Indra, the supreme divinity was invisible to the seers. But it was only Vasiṣṭha, who by the power of his penance could have the vision of Indra. As a result Indra was pleased and made the announcement that he (Vasiṣṭha) should receive shares in the soma sacrifice.[4] Since then Vasiṣṭha and his descendants began to officiate as Brhamā priests, worthy of the highest fees (दक्षिणीयतमाः).

With regard to Agastya the *Ṛgveda* speaks of his birth from the middle of the jar (ततो ह मान उदियाय मध्यात्-RV.VII.33.13.

Designated as Māna Agastya takes away Vasiṣṭha from the celestial clan and introduces him to the human society. The *BD* directly refers to the sage Agastya and instead of calling him Māna, introduces him as Mānya either because he was Śamyāmātra (being the length of a peg) or because he was produced from a jar which is used as a measure of capacity (*Bṛhaddevatā* V. 153, P. 62). A change in the nomenclature of Agastya and the anecdote of Vasiṣṭha's penance leading to his promotion to the post of Brahmā are the two conspicuous additions to the *Ṛgvedic* myth of Agastya and Vasiṣṭha.

Sarvānukramaṇī : The *Ṛgveda* Sarvānukramaṇī (1.166) in course of introducing the Agastya hymns speaks of the divine birth of Agastya and Vasiṣṭha when at the sight of Urvaśī the semen of Mitra and Vasiṣṭha fell into a jar containing water that stood overnight. There is no addition, no elaboration.

Epics and Purāṇa-Texts

When we come to the age of the Epics, we notice that very often the great epic *Mahābhārata* refers to Vasiṣṭha as the mind-born son of Brahman.[5] Apart from it, when Bhīṣma expounds the greatness of Srī-Kṛṣṇa (*Mahābhārata* XIII.143.18a), he says that it is Kṛṣṇa who gave birth to the old seer Vasiṣṭha (स कुम्भरेता ससृजे पुराणं यत्रोत्पन्नं ऋषिं आहुः वसिष्ठम्) "It is He (Kṛṣṇa) who caused the vital seed (of the gods Mitra and Varuṇa) to fall within a jar, whence sprang the sage known by the name of Vasiṣṭha". The other Epic *Rāmāyaṇa* ignores the myth as available in the popular editions of the text.

After the Epics we come to the *Purāṇa Pañcalakṣaṇa* text. Kirfel has made quite a deep study of the Purāṇas. In order to find out the urkern of the Purāṇas, he has depended upon the five chief characteristics. These five characteristics known as *Sarga, Pratisarga, Manvantara, Vaṃśa, Vaṃśānucarita* form the kernal of the Purāṇa-texts. The different Purāṇas, as are available at present have rather expanded and elaborated the subjects referred to in this *pañcalakṣaṇa-text*. Different topics like festi- vals, rituals, glorification of different gods and goddesses or holy places are definitely additions of later age. Therefore before analysing the different Purāṇas it is better to go through the common basic text of all the Purāṇas available at present. Thus *Purāṇa-Pañcalakṣaṇa* by W. Kirfel is the compilation where the original texts of the Purāṇas have been put in a chronological order. With the *Purāṇa-Pañca-lakṣaṇa* text as the base, it is better to begin our investigation of history of these two sages.

In course of giving an account of the genealogy of the king Nimi the *Vaṃśānucarita* text (p. 338.984) refers to the curse of Vasiṣṭha in consequence of which Nimi, son of Ikṣvāku, was disembodied from his self. And this Nimi founded the dynasty of Videha in which line ruled kings like Mithi (Janaka), Udāvasu and Nandivardhana, etc.

In giving an account of the genealogy of Yadu race the *Pañcalakṣaṇa* text (P. 410-418) speaks of Arjuna, the son of Kṛtavīrya when the king was on the summit of his glory and prosperity, and the subjects led a happy life under the righteous administration of the king, Lord Agni approached Kārtavīrya as a suppliant. When the king donated him all the seven continents, Agni very much hungry burnt down all these continents, including the hermitage of the revered sage Vasiṣṭha. Enraged at this Vasiṣ ṭha, also called Āpava who got the blissful birth as the son of Varuṇa (यं लेभे वरुणः पुत्रं पुरा भास्वन्तमुत्तमम् वसिष्ठं नाम स मुनिः स्यात् आपव इत्युत-42) imprecated a curse upon Kārtavīrya to the effect that he would incur a defeat at the hands of Paraśurāma. (*Pañca-lakṣaṇa* text-418, 42).

So in the *Pañcalakṣaṇa* text, the urkern of the Purāṇa literature we just get this much information that Vasiṣṭha who was known as Āpava was the son of Varuṇa. Nimi had become disembodied from his self because of Vasiṣṭha's curse for which he became Videha and the genealogy of Videha started from him. The other king cursed by Vasiṣṭha is Kārtavīryārjuna whose defeat at the hands of Paraśurāma was predicted.

Vāyu and Brahmāṇḍa : Next we come to Purāṇa texts–*Vāyu* and *Brahmāṇḍa*. As observed by Kirfel and Pargiter both these texts are rooted in one text-kernel. And this text kernel is the oldest specimen of Purāṇa literature, having embodied in it the five characteristics of Purāṇa-*Purāṇa Pañcalakṣaṇa*. Both these texts make a passing reference to the curse of Vasiṣṭha in consequence of which Nimi was disembodied from his self (स शापेन वसिष्ठस्य विदेहः समपद्यत) (*Vāyu* 27. 3-4a, *Brahmāṇḍa* III. 64.3-4a).

The *Vāyu* and *Brahmāṇḍa* give this laconic reference to Vasiṣṭha. We do not know as to what is the motive of his curse to Nimi. Leaving apart the *Purāṇa Pañcalakṣaṇa* text, which has been treated separately as it forms the nucleus of all the Purāṇas available at present, we come to a detailed analysis of the different versions of the myth of Agastya and Vasiṣṭha as available in the popular Purāṇa literature.

Viṣṇu Purāṇa (IV.5.1-12) : The *Viṣṇu* gives an elaborate version of this story which is presented in a logical form. "King Nimi, son of Ikṣvāku institutes a sacrifice to continue for a thousand years and invites Vasiṣṭha to officiate in the sacrifice. Vasiṣṭha because of his pre-engagement with Indra for five hundred years advises Nimi to wait for sometime. After completion of the sacrifice of Indra he would take up the task of officiating in his sacrifice. The king gives no answer. With the idea that king Nimi is willing to wait, Vasiṣṭha goes to Indra and performs his sacrifice. After Indra's sacrifice is over, he returns to Nimi with a view to conducting his sacrifice for which he has already promised. In the meantime Gautama is found to be busy in conducting the sacrifice of Nimi, who himself is then asleep. At this Vasiṣṭha very much enraged and displeased pronounces a curse upon Nimi to the effect that he would be disembodied from his self. (अयं विदेहो भविष्यति). Because of inflicting a curse upon him without his (Nimi's) knowledge, Nimi in return curses Vasiṣṭha to the effect that he too would be disembodied from his self (तस्मात् तस्यापि देहः पतिष्यति). As per the curse of the king,

Vasiṣṭha loses his bodily existence and his subtle body is united with the spirits of Mitra and Varuṇa.[6] In course of time the twin divinities-Mitra and Varuṇa become passionate at the sight of the nymph Urvaśī when their semen gets effused and from that semen Vasiṣṭha is born with a different body.

In consequence of the curse of Vasiṣṭha when the sacrifice of Nimi is continuing, the king too is disembodied from his self. But the corpse of Nimi was preserved from decay by being embalmed with oils and resins. At the conclusion of sacrifice the gods appear to have their shares of the sacrifice. The priests appeal to the gods to confer a blessing on Nimi, the sacrificer. Gods are willing to restore him to bodily existence, but Nimi points to the misery of human existence and refuses to be born with a mortal body again. Once his soul has departed from the body, that should be final, and no more he would have to experience the woe of death. His desire of living in the eyes of beings was assented to by the gods. Since that time he is placed in the eyes of all living creatures (असौ अशेषभूतानां नेत्रेषु अवतारितः IV.5.18).

Bhāgavata Purāṇa (IX.13.1-13) : It is nothing new but an abridged version of *Viṣṇu*. It does not mention the name of the sage appointed by Nimi for conducting the sacrifice. And the birth of Vasiṣṭha from Urvaśī as the son of Mitra and Varuṇa is just referred to without expanding the idea of the meeting of the dual divinities with Urvaśī or the effusion of their semen. It also speaks of the fact that the dead body of Nimi is preserved from decay by applying fragrant substances and lastly when Nimi declines to have any mortal frame, by churning his body the priests produce a son as the next heir to the throne. With only thirteen verses in very precise and concise manner the legend is narrated here without any addition or elaboration.

Devī Bhāgavata (VI.Ch.14-15) : It is actually the *Devī Bhāgavata* which has assimilated all the different versions of the different Purāṇa texts; the legend has been presented in a logical systematic manner. Nimi requests his preceptor Vasiṣṭha to officiate in the sacrifice. Vasiṣṭha speaks to him of his inability at the time as he has appointment with Indra. Vasiṣṭha advises him to wait.

Nimi puts forth his point that he has collected all the materials for the sacrifice. Vasiṣṭha is his family-priest. It does not behove him to disappoint him.

With the departure of Vasiṣṭha for Indra's sacrifice, Nimi does not care for him and conducts the sacrifice with the help of Gautama. Vasiṣṭha returns from Indra and waits to meet the king who is asleep. Servants do not dare to wake him up. So Vasiṣṭha feels humiliated and curses Nimi to be disembodied.

Attendants shocked to listen to the curse of the sage wake up Nimi. Nimi pleads his innocence and appeals to his good self referring to his learning and wisdom. He charges him with his greed for *dakṣiṇā*. When his prayer for withdrawing the curse is not heeded, the king curses the sage to be disembodied.

Vasiṣṭha approaches Brahmā for help. Brahmā advises him to enter into the self of Mitra and Varuṇa. As per the command of Brahmā, Vasiṣṭha goes to the abode of Varuṇa. There his self enters into the body of Mitra and Varuṇa.

Urvaśī purposely enters into the abode of Varuṇa. Mitra and Varuṇa excited to see the beautiful nymph invite Urvaśī to remain with them. When Urvaśī remains with Mitra and Varuṇa strongly attached to them, the semen of Mitra and Varuṇa is dropped in a jar and the two ascetics-Agastya and Vasiṣṭha are born.[7]

When in course of the sacrifice, the sacrificer Nimi was cursed by Vasiṣṭha, the priests engaged in his sacrifice kept alive the body of king Nimi by chanting various *mantras*. By worshipping the body with various *mantra-śaktis* they prevented the body from decay. On the completion of the sacrifice the different divinities as prayed for by the sages and the seers came to the spot. The divinities aware of the condition of the body of the king offered him the boon of taking an excellent birth as the fruit of performing the sacrifice. But Nimi humbly replies that no more he wants to have a mortal body which is always liable to destruction. On the advice of the gods the king devotedly prays the Devī Bhagavatī. When she appears before him, the king asks of her the following boons : He would be granted the knowledge which would lead to final liberation. He would be able to reside on the top of the eyes of all the beings. (नेत्रेषु सर्वभूतानां निवासो मे भवेदिति–VI.15.18). Devī Bhagavatī grants him both these boons[8] and disappears. After the Devī vanishes, the sages churn the body of king Nimi by placing *Araṇi* on it. Then there is born a son-looking like a second Nimi. As the son is born due to the churning of the *Araṇis* (अरण्या मथनात्), the boy is named Mithi. Besides as it is born (जननात्), it is called Janaka. As the king Nimi became bereft of his body, all his descendants are known as *Videhas*.

The *Ṛgvedic* legend had brought great disgrace and discredit to the character of dual divinities-Mitra and Varuṇa. They stooped so low as they had effused their semen at the sight of the beautiful nymph Urvaśī. The *Viṣṇu Purāṇa* though maintaining the lascivious character of Mitra and Varuṇa gives a logical sequence to the birth of Vasiṣṭha. In *Ṛgveda* the semen of Mitra and Varuṇa falls outside the pitcher. The gods carry the semen in a lotus flower to Urvaśī for disposal. Thus Vasiṣṭha becomes a son of Mitra and Varuṇa born of Urvaśī but born from her mind. In this account the birth of Vasiṣṭha seems to be accidental and illogical. The *Viṣṇu Purāṇa* by introducing the story of Nimi and Vasiṣṭha explains the reason as to what led to the birth of Vasiṣṭha by Mitra and Varuṇa. In *Ṛgveda* the birth of Vasiṣṭha from Mitra and Varuṇa is designated as the first birth; and he gets his birth as a human sage when Agastya introduces him to the human society, but as per the version of the *Viṣṇu Purāṇa* Vasiṣṭha had already acquired a high position in the society. The curse came only when his position as a Brahman priest had been established. So in *Viṣṇu Purāṇa* the first and second birth of Vasiṣṭha as referred to in the *Ṛgveda* are reversed. The divine birth comes only after his birth as a human sage. As Prof. Velankar

(*Ṛgveda,* Maṇḍala VII, p. 83) points out, *Ṛgvedic* hymn 33 of maṇḍala VII " is conceived as a dialogue between Indra and the leader of the Vasiṣṭha family". The leader of the family in composing this hymn had the definite purpose of giving a glowing account of the Vedic sage Vasiṣṭha and his pre-eminence as Brahman priest. The *Viṣṇu Purāṇa* version points to the fact that the Vedic tradition (*BD V.* 156-159, *TS* III.5.2.) was still alive by 8th Century A.D. or so when the *Viṣṇu Purāṇa* was composed and the position of Vasiṣṭha as a sacrificial priest was very high. Both Indra, the Lord of gods and Nimi, the founder of a dynasty are anxious to get the services of Vasiṣṭha for their sacrifice. And when Vasiṣṭha fails to oblige Nimi, he is cursed.

In *Ṛgvedic* version Mitra and Varuṇa effused the semen and Vasiṣṭha is born. Definitely the *Viṣṇu* version makes the birth of Vasiṣṭha truly divine when it says that the subtle body of Vasiṣṭha entered that of Mitra and Varuṇa. Only after the subtle body of Vasiṣṭha had entered into the souls of the two divinities when the question of dropping the semen came, Vasiṣṭha was born.

The anecdote in the *Bṛhaddevatā* (vide Ante P. 123) referring to the vision of Indra by Vasiṣṭha through his austerities and grant of Indra to Vasiṣṭha for shares in the Soma sacrifice has been reflected in the above myth where Vasiṣṭha officiates in the sacrifice of Indra even at the cost of displeasing Nimi. The redactor of the *Viṣṇu* might have elaborated it because of the fact that it was Indra who blessed Vasiṣṭha to officiate as a Brahmā priest. And it is natural that in the capacity of a Brahmā priest he would reciprocate his good will. As we notice, the story relating to Nimi has become part and parcel of the story relating to the birth of Vasiṣṭha from Mitra and Varuṇa. It is definitely a new development of the Vedic version of the myth where Nimi had never come to the picture. At the same time we must admit that the stray reference to Vasiṣṭha cursing Nimi in *Pāñcalakṣaṇa* text (Kirfel P. 338, 984) is taken up here in detail. The other difference that comes to our notice is that in the Vedic version the birth stories of both Agastya and Vasiṣṭha were joined together and Agastya was born along with Vasiṣṭha. This version drops the birth story of Agastya.

Though the *Devī-Bhāgavata* preserves the traditional form of the legend, one very often comes across the tantric bias of the redactor of this *Upa-Purāṇa*. King Nimi performs the sacrifice for propitiating the Goddess Ambikā. Indra's sacrifice too is meant for the propitiation of the highest Śakti. The peculiar feature of *Devī-Bhāgavata* is that it is the sage Vasiṣṭha who approaches Brahmā for getting relieved of the curse. In *Viṣṇu* the gods who had come to partake of their shares in the sacrifice of Nimi accede to the latter's request of living in the eyes of beings. In *Devī-Bhāgavata* the gods present in the sacrifice advise Nimi to propitiate Devī-Bhagavati to grant him the boon of residing on the top of the eyes of all the creatures. And the Devī pleased with the prayer of Nimi grants him this boon. In *Viṣṇu* even though Nimi is dead, his corpse is preserved from decay by being embalmed with fragrant oils and resins, and it looks as if the king has just died. When the dead body is preserved with all care, the soul of Nimi meets the Gods who bless him with the boon that he would have his residence in the eyes of all the creatures. The *Bhāgavata* (IX. 13) repeats the same fact that the corpse of Nimi was preserved by embalming it with fragrant substance. But in *Devī-Bhāgavata* the question of preserving the dead body with application of artificial means does not come up. The priests officiating in the sacrifice of Nimi keep alive the body of the king by chanting various *mantras*. Moreover by adoring the body with various *mantra-Śaktis* they prevent the body from decay.

The *Viṣṇu* version relates the curse of Vasiṣṭha and Nimi to each other in a prosaic manner. It is just mechanical. Vasiṣṭha curses because Nimi has humiliated him by appointing another priest. Nimi too curses because Vasiṣṭha had cursed him without his knowledge when he was asleep. The motive of each cursing the other is same in the *Bhāgavata*. But the *Devī-Bhāgavata* rather elaborates the motive of the curse. When Vasiṣṭha returns from Indra's sacrifice, the sage Gautama had already finished the performance of the sacrifice. With bountiful gifts the priests had already returned from the sacrifice. The king Nimi was fast asleep. The servants though present did not wake him up from the sleep and the king too did not care to meet the sage. Consequently Vasiṣṭha felt insulted and cursed the king. The text in further expounding the reasons of the curse goes on : Vasiṣṭha, his life-long preceptor has been ignored. His clear direction for not beginning the sacrifice without his presence has been violated and king Nimi has been initiated in the sacrifice by sheer force. In *Viṣṇu* Nimi curses Vasiṣṭha only because he had been cursed when he was asleep. The *Bhāgavata* text too repeats this point. But the *Devī-Bhāgavata* creates the occasion for a meeting between Nimi and Vasiṣṭha. Having come to know of the curse of Vasiṣṭha, Nimi approaches the sage with all humility. Though addressing Vasiṣṭha as knower of *Dharma* (धर्मज्ञ) and declaring himself as his *Yajamāna,* he brings the charge against Vasiṣṭha that he did not care to officiate in his sacrifice, only because of the greed. Even though as the son of Brahmā, he is well-versed in Vedic lore, he has shown his ignorance of the Brahmanic religion. The argument of Nimi appears like a sermon on morality when Nimi says : anger is much disgraceful than a Caṇḍāla; the righteous should overcome it by all means.[9] Because Vasiṣṭha infuriated with rage has cursed him for absolutely no fault on his part, Nimi curses Vasiṣṭha right away. Thus as in *Viṣṇu* and *Bhāgavata,* here in *Devī-Bhāgavata* the character of Nimi is not dull and lifeless. Servants wake him up. He justifies his stand for performing the sacrifice. He appeals to the good sense of Vasiṣṭha for withdrawing the curse, he tries to prove his innocence, when all this fails, he equates Vasiṣṭha's conduct and behaviour with that of a Caṇḍāla and curses him. Thus in the *Purāṇa* we meet the king Nimi as a man of vigour, vehemence and personality. It must be admitted that the character of the king is very much life-like.

The version in *Viṣṇu Purāṇa* follows the Vedic tradition when it makes the simple statement that Vasiṣṭha was born of Mitra and Varuṇa when their semen effused because of their excitement at the sight of Urvaśī. The *Bhāgavata* presents it in a more laconic manner when it says that Vasiṣṭha was born of Urvaśī as the son of the Mitra and Varuṇa (मित्रावरुणयो: जज्ञे उर्वश्यां प्रपितामह: IX. 13.6) Unlike the versions in *Viṣṇu* and *Bhāgavata* the version in *Devī-Bhāgavata* gives a different turn to the story. After having been cursed by king Nimi Vasiṣṭha takes shelter with Brahmā. Very pathetically he appeals to Brahmā on two different counts : 1. He would like to have his birth with a body like the present one; 2. In his new birth with the body he would have the recollection of his past life. Brahmā advises him to enter the self of Mitra and Varuṇa. Accordingly Vasiṣṭha proceeds to the abode of Varuṇa where his self enters into the body of Mitra and Varuṇa. In the meantime Urvaśī comes to the residence of Varuṇa. The two divinities Mitra and Varuṇa request Urvaśī to put up with them. Urvaśī agrees to the proposal. In course of time when Urvaśī begins to remain there strongly attached to them, the semen of Mitra and Varuṇa is dropped in a jar and the two ascetics-Agastya and Vasiṣṭha are born.

In *Viṣṇu* without the direction or guidance of any God or Goddess the self of Vasiṣṭha is united with the self of Mitra and Varuṇa. When they are excited at the sight of Urvaśī, there is the birth of Vasiṣṭha to the exclusion of the sage Agastya. The *Bhāgavata* too speaks of Vasiṣṭha "reborn of Urvaśī as the son of Mitra and Varuṇa". Unlike these two texts, the *Devī-Bhāgavata* refers to Urvaśī residing in the company of Mitra and Varuṇa. When she remains strongly attached to them, the semen of Mitra and Varuṇa is dropped in a jar and the two ascetics are born. Agastya is the first child and Vasiṣṭha the second child. In all the three texts there are two divinities who drop their semen. But in *Viṣṇu* and *Bhāgavata* in spite of the parentage of both Mitra and Varuṇa it is only Vasiṣṭha who is born. But in *Devī-Bhāgavata* in conformity with the parentage of Mitra and Varuṇa the two sages-Agastya and Vasiṣṭha are born. And Vasiṣṭha is the younger of the two.

Another point is the peculiarity of the birth of Vasiṣṭha. The *Viṣṇu* never speaks of the physical union of the twin divinities with the nymph Urvaśī. As the text puts it, through the passion of Mitra and Varuṇa for Urvaśī, the sage is born again in a different shape. (अर्वशीदर्शनात् उद्[illegible]बीजप्रपातयोस्तयोः सकाशात् वसिष्ठो देहमपरं लेभे) Though the *Bhāgavata* presents a concise version of the *Viṣṇu*, it seems, the redactor of the *Bhāgavata* has not cared to drop the physical union of Mitra and Varuṇa with Urvaśī. The text of *Bhāgavata* reads : "Great-grand father (Vasiṣṭha) is reborn of Urvaśī as the son of Mitra and Varuṇa". (मित्रावरुणयोर्जज्ञे उर्वश्यां प्रपितामहः) The *Devī-Bhāgavata* is very clear on keeping apart the twin divinities and Urvaśī. In order to emphasise this point that Agastya and Vasiṣṭha are born from the semen dropped in a jar, and not from the womb of Urvaśī, the *Devī-Bhāgavata* puts one extra boon in blessings of Brahmā. Vasiṣṭha had asked for two things : 1. taking a birth with the old body 2. retaining the recollections of the past life. Besides conferring these two boons asked for by Vasiṣṭha Brahmā blesses him that in due time he would get a body not born of any womb. In keeping with the old Vedic tradition the *Devī-Bhāgavata* puts this peculiar birth of Agastya and Vasiṣṭha (who are born from the semen dropped in a jar) among the three boons of Brahmā. Brahmā blesses the sage Vasiṣṭha : "You will be born not of any womb" (तस्मादयोनिजः काले भविता त्वं न संशयः).

Besides elaborating on different aspects of the myth preserved in *Viṣṇu*, the *Devī-Bhāgavata* is rather critical on the question of Vasiṣṭha cursing Nimi and Nimi cursing Vasiṣṭha. The text (Part-I. 19) raises a pertinent issue as to how Nimi who had been earlier cursed by Vasiṣṭha to be disembodied could remain alive to curse Vasiṣṭha. The text solves this ticklish problem with the statement that the soul of Nimi, even though bereft of body was still endowed with the five elements like earth, water, fire, air and ether.[10]

Matsya Purāṇa (Ch. 200) : The *Matsya Purāṇa*11 gives a new turn to this story. Vasiṣṭha is engaged as the officiating priest in the sacrifices conducted under the patronage of Nimi. Quite a number of sacrifices are performed, Vasiṣṭha feels tired and exhausted. In the meantime Nimi approaches Vasiṣṭha to conduct some more sacrifices on his behalf. The sage very humbly replies that he would begin the sacrifice only after he feels recouped. At this reply of the sage, king Nimi gives a long discourse on the frailty of human life (*ślokas* 6-12). The king says the last word that if Vasiṣṭha would not come forward for officiating in his sacrifice, he would get it performed through some other priest. Very much hurt by these unkind words, Vasiṣṭha pronounces the curse upon Nimi–"you want to get rid of me; and you propose to appoint another priest, when I am feeling so tired and exhausted; be devoid of your bodily form."[12] The king in return curses the sage in these words–"you too become devoid of your bodily form because you are an obstacle in the path of my righteousness". In consequence of the curse both the sage and the king are bereft of their bodies, and their souls go to Lord Brahmā. Brahmā, the primeval father of all the beings protects both of them. He gives the foremost place to Nimi by advising him to be constantly present in the eyes of all the creatures.[13] The sage Vasiṣṭha is consoled with the blessings that he would be born as the son of Mitra and Varuṇa. Then he would be known by his old name Vasiṣṭha. Besides he would have recollection of his previous birth. (जन्मद्वयमतीतं च तत्रापि त्वं स्मरिष्यसि, Chapt. 200).

Once upon a time it so happens that in the hermitage Badarikā Mitra and Varuṇa are engaged in practising penance. When the spring season had given a new colour to the surroundings, Mitra and Varuṇa catch sight of Urvaśī, the paragon of beauty dressed in a fine attire of red colour. Both the sages greatly agitated at the sight of this divine beauty drop their semen on the skin of a deer. Afraid of a curse from Urvaśī both the sages[14] collect the semen in a pitcher full of water. And out of it are born the sages-Agastya and Vasiṣṭha.

On a comparative analysis of the two legends in the *Devī–Bhāgavata* and *Matsya,* in the *Devī–Bhāgavata* the dispute arises when Nimi's request for starting the sacrifice immediately is not heeded by Vasiṣṭha. Nimi very fervently pleads for his cause. Vasiṣṭha returns from Indra with the hope of beginning the sacrifice of Nimi, but as the text reads, there was no justification for Vasiṣṭha to return to Nimi as the latter had never assured that he would wait. Vasiṣṭha's curse to Nimi is rather unwarranted. Even after Vasiṣṭha had imprecated the curse, Nimi does not retaliate immediately. With patience and sincerity he refers to the status and dignity of the sage. It would not be befitting for him to curse the innocent king. Of course, sometimes we find, the king has crossed the bounds of decency when he charges the revered sage with his greed for *dakṣiṇā*. Nimi's curse to Vasiṣṭha comes only when the sage remains firm and does not withdraw the curse.

On the other hand the *Matsya Purāṇa* version of the legend is rather interesting. There is no question of Vasiṣṭha officiting in the sacrifice of Indra. From the very beginning the illustrious sage is busy in performing a number of sacrifices for Nimi. Naturally he is tired and exhausted. Therefore, it is quite unjust for the king to force him for performing some more sacrifices. Naturally here in this legend of *Matsya*, Vasiṣṭha draws our sympathy, when he pronounces the curse upon Nimi. In the same way one can't find fault with Nimi, if one takes into account the solid ground and vigorous argument that he has put forward for continuing the sacrifice without delay. In eight verses[15] (5-12) the king presents a vivid picture of death and uncertainties of life. The redactor of *Matsya* has done a nice job of presenting both the characters–the king and the sage in a lively manner. In face of the argument of the sage that Nimi should wait for sometime because he is tired and exhausted, we have the counter argument of the king–"Righteous deeds must be performed immediately; there is no certainty of life". The argument of Vasiṣṭha is equally valid like the forceful discourse of the king. Each curses the other. The reader is actually in a fix as to who is to blame.

Thus we notice that in *Devī Bhāgavata* Vasiṣṭha is presented as a sage very much comparable to Durvāsas. Inspite of being implored with convincing arguments Vasiṣṭha never relents. In

Matsya both the king and the sage stand on an equal footing. In sketching the character of the sage and the king the redactor of *Matsya* has done a fine job. The reader fails to find any flaw in the stand taken by either of the two. In *Devī Bhāgavata* the point of dispute is Vasiṣṭha's preference for officiating in the sacrifice of Indra; in *Matsya* the bone of contention is not that the sage disappoints Nimi for the sake of Indra, but rather it is a question of giving opportunity to Vasiṣṭha to rest and relax.

Both the versions are almost identical in the development of the legend after each curses the other. The only extra favour (?), if it can be called a favour of blessing Vasiṣṭha to have his birth not from any Womb noted in *Devī Bhāgavata,* has been dropped altogether in Matsya. Otherwise their refuge in Brahmā and the boons granted by the primal father are almost the same.

In *Devī Bhāgavata* the twin divinites Mitra and Varuṇa do not conduct themselves in keeping with their position as celestials. Like ordinary human beings hit by the arrows of Cupid, they run after Urvaśī. After Urvaśī has spent some days in the company of Mitra and Varuṇa, their semen is dropped in a jar (vide the extra favour of Brahmā that Vasiṣṭha would be *ayonija*) and there is the birth of Agastya and Vasiṣṭha. On the other hand in *Matsya* (Ch. 200) the passion and excitement noticed in the character of Mitra and Varuṇa is not something so despicable. For the redactor of *Matsya* Mitra and Varuṇa are two sages practising penance. Like so many sages who have fallen from the height of their glory at the sight of some lovely damsel or heavenly nymph, these two sages are excited to see Urvaśī. In the *Devī Bhāgavata* "dropping of the semen in the jar" is maintained in keeping with the Vedic tradition. *Matsya* makes the semen drop on the skin of the deer, seated on which they are practising penance. It is more natural and realistic; but at the same time we must admit that the redactor of *Matsya* has not shown the sign of good taste when he makes the two sages collect their own semen dropped on the skin of the deer and then deposit it in a pitcher. In both the versions though only Vasiṣṭha was blessed by Brahmā to be born as the son of Mitra and

Varuṇa, Agastya too takes his birth along with him. None of these versions gives the reason as to how Agastya could have his birth along with Vasiṣṭha but though the texts have not supplied us with any information about the antecedents of Agastya, we must remain satisfied with the fact that the Purāṇa texts closely followed the Vedic tradition.

Conclusion

In the different Purāṇa texts reviewed uptil now we notice that Agastya and Vasiṣṭha are born from the semen dropped by Mitra and Varuṇa. Introduction of the curse of Nimi to Vasiṣṭha is the antecedent for which Vasiṣṭha takes his birth from Mitra and Varuna. In the Vedic texts without assigning any reason there is the plain statement that Agastya and Vasiṣṭha are born. The Purāṇa texts like *Viṣṇu, Bhāgavata, Devī Bhāgavata, Matsya* and *Viṣṇu-dharmottara* developed only a part of the legend when they justified the birth of Vasiṣṭha by introducing the curse of Nimi but the question of Agastya went unnoticed. For the first time here in the *Matsya* Ch. 61 we find that Agastya has been born from Mitra and Varuṇa for which there is a definite cause.

Matsya (Ch. 61) *version of the story*[16] : This text introduces the story of the mythical fight between the gods and the demons. The demons taking shelter inside the waters of the ocean continue troubling the gods and the sages again and again. At this Indra, the Lord of gods directs Fire and Wind to dry up the ocean. Both Fire and Wind refuse to carry out the command of Indra, as in their opinion drying up the ocean would lead to the destruction of innumerable beings taking shelter in its waters. With his order flouted both Fire and Wind are cursed to be born jointly by assuming one body among the mortals in the form of the sage Agastya. In consequence of the curse both Fire and Wind come down to the earth; and they are jointly born out of the pitcher by the semen of Mitra and Varuṇa and come to be known as Agastya, the younger brother of Vasiṣṭha.[17]

The motive of the birth of Vasiṣṭha. is retained as before. Nimi curses Vasiṣṭha.. who takes refuge in Brahmā. Brahmā blesses Vasiṣṭha that he would be born from Mitra and Varuṇa. Thus the text gives a connected whole with reference to the curses leading to the birth of Agastya and Vasiṣṭha.

After these two sages are imprecated with a curse, the *Matsya* gives a new turn to the story. Viṣṇu, son of Dharma practises penance on the summit of the Gandhamādana mountain. Indra, terribly afraid of it sends a group of nymphs to disturb and destroy his penance. Viṣṇu unmoved by these distractions produces from his thigh the nymph Urvaśī,[18] a damsel of exquisite beauty. Gods become enamoured of her. Then Mitra requests her for co-habitation and she gives her consent. Next in a passionate mood lustful Varuṇa pulls her by the hem of her garment. But Urvaśī tells him that already she had come to be the wife of Mitra and naturally she could not be his wife again. When Varuṇa prayed her to keep him in her favour, Urvaśī assented. Mitra coming to know of Urvaśī's favour to Varuṇa cursed her to be born among the mortals and get married to Budha, the son of the moon because of behaving like a courtezan. Just then both Mitra and Varuṇa drop their semen in a pitcher of water out of which Agastya and Vasiṣṭha are born.

Out of the three different versions of the myth, in the first version[19] it is only Agastya who is born from the semen of Mitra and Varuṇa though the particular text refers to Agastya as younger brother of Vasiṣṭha. But the common parentage of Agastya and Vasiṣṭha is clearly presented in the two other versions.[20]

In the texts both Vedic and Purāṇic we have reviewed uptil now nowhere there is any reference as to how and why Agastya could have his birth from the semen of Mitra and Varuṇa. *Viṣṇu* and *Matsya* (Ch. 200) gave the reason for the birth of Vasiṣṭha from Mitra and Varuṇa. It is only the *Matsya* (Ch. 61)[21] which logically analysed the events leading to the birth of Agastya from Mitra and Varuṇa. In *Matsya* (Ch. 200) the Purāṇa-text just narrates the fact that Mitra and Varuṇa, engaged in practising penance, are enamoured at the sight of Urvaśī and from their semen Agastya and Vasiṣṭha are born. But the *Matsya* (Ch. 61) dramatically presents the union of the dual divinities-Mitra and Varuṇa with Urvaśī. Viṣṇu practises penance. Indra deputes nymphs to disturb his penance. Viṣṇu befools Indra by producing Urvaṣī from his thigh. Then Mitra requests Urvaṣī for co-habitation and she gives her consent. Later Varuṇa pulls her by her attaire. There arises a dispute between the two. Mitra curses Urvaṣī to be born on earth and then only Vasiṣṭha and Agastya are born when the divinities let their semen drop in a jar. As in *Devī-Bhāgavata* here in this text Mitra and Varuṇa come face to face with Urvaśī when Mitra's co-habitation is clearly mentioned, and Varuṇa's is suggested.[22] Naturally the Vedic reference to Vasiṣṭha as a son of Mitra and Varuṇa born from the mind of Urvaśī is totally ignored. The same is the case with Agastya. But in keeping with the Vedic tradition the redactor all at once makes the statement that Mitra and Varuṇa had their semen dropped in a pitcher of water, from which both the sages were born. On the other hand Urvaśī asserts before Varuṇa–"मित्रेणाहं वृता पूर्वमद्य" but still then when she assents to Varuṇa's request to keep him in her favour, Mitra curses her as वेश्याधर्म एष त्वया कृतः।

The next point of difference of *Matsya* (Ch. 61) from the preceding texts (like *Viṣṇu, Matsya* Ch. 200) relates to the feud between Nimi and Vasiṣṭha. In *Viṣṇu* Vasiṣṭha's partiality for Indra leads to his curse by Nimi. In *Matsya* Ch. 200 Indra does not come to picture. It is Nimi's insistence for preforming the sacrifice when Vasiṣṭha is tired and exhausted that results in Nimi's curse to Vasiṣṭha. This particular text *Matsya* (Ch. 61) alludes to a very common and popular motif of the curse. Nimi is engaged in the game of dice with women. Vasiṣṭha happens to be there. Nimi fails to give due regard to Vasiṣṭha. In consequence Vasiṣṭha curses Nimi and Nimi in retaliation curses Vasiṣṭha. Unlike these versions of *Viṣṇu* and *Matsya* Ch. 200 this text is rather dull and dry. The reader may find some justification for the curse Vasiṣṭha. One may remember in *Viṣṇu,* Vasiṣṭha had cursed Nimi when he was asleep. That is why Nimi had retaliated. In *Matsya* Ch. 200 Nimi had cursed Vasiṣṭha because the latter happened to be an obstacle in his sacrifice. Of these three texts relating to the episode of curse of both Nimi and Vasiṣṭha to each other, this text Ch. 200 is most interesting from the point that both the king and the sage stand on a sound footing for cursing each other. In that point the version of *Matsya* Ch. 61 is the least logical where Nimi curses Vasiṣṭha just in a mechanical way.

The *Narmasiṃha Purāṇa*[23] has no claim to be regarded as a Mahāpurāṇa. The Vaiṣṇava Upa-Purāṇa like *Viṣṇudharma, Viṣṇudharmottara* and *Narmasiṃha Purāṇa* are of quite early origin : these texts enjoy very wide reputation as respectable authorities on *Dharma.* Particularly or specially the *Narmasiṃha Purāṇa* translated into Telugu about 1300 A.D. is profusely drawn upon by the commentators and Nivandha writers both early and late. Vallālasena who is very cautious in utilising the different Purāṇas for his *Dānasāgara* rejects Purāṇas like "*Garuḍa, Brahma, Āngeya, Vaiṣṇava* and *Liṅga* as spurious. On the other hand he draws upon the *Narmasiṃha Purāṇa* without the least shade of doubt as regards its authenticity, antiquity and non-tantric character". Hazra is of opinion that by the first half of the 11th century A.D. *Narmasiṃha Purāṇa* had attained a pre-eminent position.

In *Narmasiṃha Purāṇa* (Ch.6)[24] Varuṇa is no more just an Āditya. As the guardian of the quarters he presides over the western sea. On the peak of Śaileśa-a beautiful golden mountain there is the city Viśvāvatī fashioned by Viśvakarman. Directed by Brahmā the Āditya Varuṇa stationed in this city protects all these worlds. Gandharvas and heavenly damsels use to attend upon him. Once upon a time Varuṇa in the company of Mitra besmeared with divine fragrant substance goes to the lovely sacred place Kurukṣetra and both of them practise penance there. In the forest region of Kurukṣetra there lies a beautiful lake "Pauṇḍarīka" by name. Once they go for a stroll and come across Urvaśī who is taking her bath in the lake. In six verses (26-33) *Narmasiṃha Purāṇa* gives a glowing description of the matchless beauty of Urvaśī–her lotus like lustre, glossy dark tresses of hair, wide expansive eyes, lovely nose, slender waist, handsome arms and feet. On the whole she appears like a full moon with the gait of an elephant. Added to the amorous gestures of Urvaśī who used to sing in sweet melodious voice, there blows the sweet fragrant breeze, the surrounding resounds with the humming of the bees and the sweet note of the cuckoos. Thus when the stage is all set for the full flash, Urvaśī casts her side long glances at Mitra and Varuṇa. Mitra and Varuṇa greatly agitated and excited effuse their semen. The self of Vasiṣṭha who has been disembodied by the curse of Nimi takes refuge in the semen emitted by these two gods. The Viśvedevāḥ appear there and make a prophecy that Vasiṣṭha would be born as the son of Mitra and Varuṇa. And it is also approved by Brahmā. The seminal fluid lies scattered in three different places-the lotus, the land and the water. From the semen deposited in the lotus is born Vasiṣṭha; from the semen scattered in land Agastya is born and from the semen deposited in the water, the Fish of great effulgence (जले मत्स्यो महाद्युति:).[25] In the meantime Urvaśī leaves for heaven. The twin-gods Mitra and Varuṇa along with the sages Vasiṣṭha and Agastya come back to their hermitage and continue their rigorous penance as before. Brahmā comes there and informs the two divinities that they have been blessed with progeny. They would attain further favours from Viṣṇu. They should remain firm in their position (and practise austerities as before). Having said so Brahmā disappears.

In analysis of the myth of the *Narmasiṃha Purāṇa* given above, we are surprised to find that the myth of Agastya and Vasiṣṭha given in all its details with its ancedotes in *Matsya* (Ch. 61) and *Padma* (I.22) has been presented here in a short simple way. The myth relates to the central concept of the *Ṛgvedic* Sūkta 7.33.9-14. The earlier versions of the myth in the Purāṇa texts presented the dispute between Nimi and Vasiṣṭha in the most interesting and dramatic manner. This particular anecdote is totally ignored with but a slight reference to Nimi's curse (मुने: शापादथोत्क्रम्य स्वदेहान्मुनिसत्तम)–The reason for dropping out the curse stories may be traced to the fact that the myth of the miraculous birth of Agastya and Vaisiṣṭha has been recounted in this Purāṇa text with the sole purpose of enabling people to be blessed with male progeny. The *phalaśruti* of the chapter states that this legend of *Puṃsavana*[26] (the rite through which a male child is born) relating to Varuṇa is destroyer of all sins. Those persons who desirous of getting male children lead a righteous life and listen to this particular legend, very soon are favoured with the birth of sons; there is no doubt in it.[27] Naturally the curse story relating to Nimi and Vasiṣṭha, the feud between Indra on one hand and Fire and Wind on the other have become irrelevant.

In all the preceding texts after the birth of Agastya and Vasiṣṭha the reader fails to find that love and affection which one expects from a father. Mitra and Varuṇa are unconcerned about their progeny. But in this text Mitra and Varuṇa guide their sons to their hermitage and the birth of Agastya and Vasiṣṭha is referred to by Brahmā as a favour. And for primal father Brahmā the fatherhood of Agastya and Vasiṣṭha is a great achievement for the twin divinities (मित्रवरुणकौ देवौ पुत्रवन्तौ महाद्युती).

In *Narmasiṃha Purāṇa* we see Varuṇa[28] in a new form. He is the guardian of western quarters. Directed by Brahmā Varuṇa protects all these worlds. In the city Viśvāvatī the great celestial city of gold situated on Śaileśa (the Lord of mountains), Varuṇa shines there in all his splendour. The preceding Purāṇa texts refer to Varuṇa as an *āditya*, just one of the twelve *ādityas* born of Aditi by Kaśyapa. By referring to Varuṇa as a Lokapāla, a position of authority the *Narmasiṃha Purāṇa* has given a new turn to his position and status. He is subservient only to Brahmā, who occupies the foremost position in the hierarchy of the gods.

The question of Varuṇa ruling over the western quarters with his residence in the most gorgeous city of Viśvāvatī going to practise penance in the company of Mitra appears inconsistent. The Purāṇa fails to adduce any motive for the king to leave the throne and to go to the forest for practising penance. But still then under the influence of *Matsya* (Ch. 200) and *Viṣṇudharmottara* (Part-I.117) the *Narmasiṃha Purāṇa* retains the old motive-meeting of Urvaśī at the time of penance. The two divinities Mitra and Varuṇa come across Urvaśī in the forest where they are practising penance. But the difference is that in the *Narmasiṃha* text Varuṇa abandons his regal mansion along with all its attendant pleasures and leaves for the forest. In both the texts (*Matsya* ch. 200, *Viṣṇudharmottara* I.117) Mitra and Varuṇa engaged in penance in the hermitage Badarikā catch sight of Urvaśī when she is busy in plucking flowers. It is a fitting situation no doubt to make the union of Mitra and Varuṇa agitated and excited. Urvaśī comes to the notice of the two divinities when she is singing and smiling, her physical beauty and charm is exposed to them in its entirety.

In *Ṛgveda* the semen of Mitra and Varuṇa had fallen in an earthern pitcher and partly outside it, from which Agastya and Vasiṣṭha were respectively born. The *Bṛhaddevatā* makes both the ascetics born from their semen after it had dropped in a jar. The *Viṣṇu Purāṇa* ignores the question of birth of Agastya and follows the *Ṛgveda* in the statement that Vasiṣṭha was born from the semen after it had dropped; but in order to justify the birth of Vasiṣṭha the *Viṣṇu Purāṇa* is consistent in so far as in the preceding sentence it has referred to the fact that the soul of Vasiṣṭha who had already become disembodied because of the curse of Nimi, had taken refuge in the semen of Mitra and Varuṇa (तत् शापाच्च मित्रबरुणयोस्तेजसि वसिष्ठस्य चेतः प्रविष्टम्). The *Matsya* (Ch. 200) unlike *Viṣṇu* does not give the prior information that the soul of Vasiṣṭha has taken refuge with Mitra and Varuṇa. But the story does not appear so incongruous or inconsistent. After referring to the blessings of Brahmā that Vasiṣṭha would be born from Mitra and Varuṇa, the former has its birth from their semen when it drops. In *Matsya* Ch. 61 the self of Vasiṣṭha after he is disembodied goes to Brahmā and as per the order of Brahmā Vasiṣṭha is born of the pitcher which contained the semen of Mitra and Varuna. In *Devī-Bhāgavata* the self of Vasiṣṭha as directed by Brahmā had entered the *tejas* of Mitra and Varuṇa and when their semen had effused, from there along with Agastya Vasiṣṭha was born.[29] Of all the Purāṇa-texts it is only *Narasiṃha* which has rather pulled down Vasiṣṭha from his dignified celestial status. Only after the semen of Mitra and Varuṇa had dropped when they were agitated at the sight of Urvaśī, the self of Vasiṣṭha leaves its mortal body and enters into the semen. Further the *Narasiṃha Purāṇa* speaks of the three divisions of the semen in three different places-lotus, land, and water (स्कन्दतस्तावुभावपि निमे: शापादथोत्क्रम्य स्वदेहान्मुनिसत्तम 6.33).

In *Ṛgveda,* like all the myths this myth of the birth of Agastya and Vasiṣṭha is given in a laconic and fragmentary manner. The different Purāṇa-texts in presenting the myth analyse, elaborate and give the pros and cons of the myth. But on one point all the Purāṇa texts agree-sudden break in the continuity of the story when the question of the real birth of Agastya and Vasiṣṭha comes. In *Matsya* (Ch. 61) and *Padma* (I.22) immediately after Urvaśī has been cursed by Mitra because she dangled before Varuṇa, the semen of Mitra and Varuṇa got effused. Inspite of Varuṇa's absence near Urvaśī and Mitra's wrathful state of mind, the *Matsya* and *Padma* make the dual divinites-Mitra and Varuṇa drop their semen. In *Devī-Bhāgavata* (VI.14) Mitra and Varuṇa had the company of Urvaśī in their residence. When the beautiful Urvaśī remained there strongly attached to them (गृहीत्वा तु तयोर्भावं संस्थिता चारुदर्शना), the semen of Mitra and Varuṇa dropped. But *Narasiṃha Purāṇa* does not speak of Urvaśī living with Mitra or Varuṇa. Urvaśī is taking bath in a lake. Just when Urvaśī casts her side glances at Mitra and Varuṇa, they drop their semen.

In other Purāṇa-texts Brahmā appeared to help Vasiṣṭha in his predicament. He had done a favour to Vasiṣṭha in directing him to be born from Mitra and Varuṇa. Otherwise Brahmā himself had nothing to do with Mitra and Varuṇa. But here in the *Narasiṃha Purāṇa* Mitra and Varuṇa appear as if they are the protege of the creator. After the birth of Vasiṣṭha Brahmā comes to these two prominent divinities when they are practising austerities (तपस्यन्तौ सुरश्रेष्ठौ) and congratulates them–"You two divinities, Mitra and Varuṇa have now been blessed with sons of great effulgence. As the witness of the three worlds you remain firm in your position (and continue your austerities) so that you will attain further blessings of Viṣṇu.[30]"

Thus the developments of the story of the birth of Vasiṣṭha and Agastya has been shown phase by phase right from the *Ṛgveda* to the latest *Upa-Purāṇa.* These two divine sages Agastya and Vasiṣṭha have been immortalised in the cultural tradition of our country. They are the teachers of divine wisdom, and their contribution to the growth and development of our religious thought is quite significant. In the assembly of the sages Vasiṣṭha held such an enviable position that a demon assumed the form of the sage and posed himself as Vasiṣṭha.[31] In the drama *Veṇīsaṃhāra* Karṇa has left the battle field in panic. Aśvatthāmā reprimands him for his cowardly nature alluding to his birth in the line of charioteers. स्तुतिवंशकीर्तनविदां सारथीनां कुले (III.35). At this caustic remark of Aśvatthāmā Karṇa gives a pertinent reply when he says: "charioteer or charioteer's son let me be what I am. Birth in a family is due to providence whereas valour is due to myself."[32] The *Vajrasūcī Upaniṣad,* one of the later Upaniṣads belonging to Sāmaveda vehemently argues against the difference of this caste, creed and colour and asserts that it is one's own virtues that count, not the birth. In justifying the statement the text[33] gives a pointed reference to Vasiṣṭha and Agastya, who not withstanding their birth from Urvaśī or from a pitcher have sacred unique position among the sages because of their knowledge and wisdom. In keeping with the glorious tradition of our land India has secured a unique position in the comity of nations as a secular State where difference of caste, creed or colour has been totally ignored.

References

1. The seven sages representing the constellation called Ursa Major are Mārīci, Atrī, Aṅgiras, Pulastya, Pulaha, Kratu and Vasiṣṭha.
2. By *Puṣkara* Yāska does not mean the lotus. Instead he attributes three other different meanings to it : (*a*) atmosphere (*b*) Water (*c*) Lotus.

3. In giving the logical sequence of the story the lines (151,152 first half. p. 62) in the text *Bṛhaddevatā* have been purposely ignored. In editing the BD Macdonell refers to two groups of manuscripts A and B and he is of opinion that the manuscripts of A group are more correct than those of the B group. And the three lines referred to above belong to the B group. As the learned author himself says, "we have a later addition in these three lines". The story as developed in these three lines appears somewhat disconnected. In the preceding verse 149 when it is clearly said that the semen of Mitra and Varuṇa fell into a jar, here it is said that the semen fell in various ways-in a jar, in water and on ground. Agastya was produced from the jar, Matsya was produced from the waters and Vasiṣṭha was produced on the ground.
4. This special privilege accorded to Vasiṣṭha by Indra is primarily traced in the *TS* III 5.2.
5. *Mahābhārata*-I 174.5, II 11, 18-19, III. 31.12, VII 6.6, XII. 166.15-1.6,
6. तत् शापाच्च मित्रावरुणयोस्तेजसि वसिष्ठस्य चेतः प्रविष्टम्।
उर्वशीदर्शनात् उद्भूतबीजप्रपातयोस्तयोः सकाशात् वसिष्ठो देहमपरं लेभे।
Viṣnu Purāṇa, IV 5.12.
7. विहरस्व यथाकामं स्थानेऽस्मिन् वरवर्णिनि।
तथोक्ता सा ततो देवी ताभ्यां तत्र स्थिता वशा।।63।।
कृत्वा भावं स्थिरं देवी मित्रावरुणयोः गृहे।
सा गृहीत्वा तयोः भावं संस्थिता चारुदर्शना।।64।।
8. ज्ञानं ते विमलं भूयात् प्रारब्धस्यविशेषतः।।19।।
नेत्रेषु सर्वभूतानां निवासोऽपि भविष्यति।।20।।
9. त्याज्यस्तु सुजनैः क्रोधश्चण्डालादधिको यतः।
तथा क्रोधपरीतेन मयि शापः प्रपातितः। *Devī Bhāgavata* VI. 14, 49.
10 *Devī Bhāgavata,* Book I.19 महाभूतानि सर्वत्र निःसंगः क्व भविष्यसि।
Devī Bhāgavata, I. 19. 30.
11. The version of *Matsya* is almost identical with the version of *Viṣṇudharmottara* (Part I.117)
12. श्रान्तं मां त्वं समुत्सृज्य यस्मादन्यं द्विजोत्तमम्। धर्मज्ञस्तु नरेन्द्र त्वं याजकं कर्तुमिच्छसि। *Matsya Purāṇa* Ch. 200. 14-15
13. अद्यप्रभृति ते स्थानं निमिजीव ददाम्यहम्।
नेत्रपक्ष्मसु सर्वेषां त्वं वसिष्यसि पार्थिव।
त्वत्सम्बन्धात्तथा तेषां निमेषः सम्भविष्यति।। *Matsya Purāṇa*-Ch. 200. 18-19

14 The only difference between *Matsya* and *Viṣṇudharmottara* is on this point that in the latter afraid of a curse it is Urvaśī who herself collects the semen of Mitra and Varuṇa.

15. The stanzas numbering 5 to 12 because of the ennobling and glorifying ideas contained in it deserve a place in the ascetic literature of Sanskrit.

16. The version of *Matsya* (Ch. 61) is almost identical with that of *Padma* (I.22).

17. मित्रावरुणयोर्वीर्याद् वसिष्ठस्यानुजोऽभवत्।
अगस्त्य इत्युग्रतपाः सम्बभूव पुनर्मुनिः॥61.19॥

18. Yāska in giving the etymological meaning of the word Urvaśī says: Urvaśī is a nymph (so called because she pervades the wide regions (Uru +...*aś* "to pervade") or she pervades by means of thighs (Uru +... *aś* "to pervade") or her desire is great (Uru aś "to pervade") or her desire is great (Uru Vaś "to desire") उर्वशी अप्सरा, उर्वभ्यः अश्नुते, ऊरुभ्यां अश्नुते, ऊरुर्वा वशोऽस्याः The *Bṛhaddevatā* in II. 59 refers to Urvaśī as Uruvāsinī. In this etymological explanation of the word, the *BD* differs from any of the three derivations given in the *Nirukta* पुरूरवसमाह एनं स्ववाक्येन ऊरुवासिनी "Uruvāsinī (Urvaśī) in her own words calls him Purūravas." It might be that Yāska's derivation of Urvaśī (ऊरुभ्यामश्नुते, she pervades by means of thighs) or *Bṛhaddevata's* reference to Urvaśī as Uruvāsinī might have prompted the redactors of the Purāṇas to connect the birth of Urvaśī with *Uru* and to develop a myth out of it. *Mahābhārata,* Ādiparvan Ch. 169-170 speaks of a divine sage Aurva who was born after tearing open the thigh of his mother (स और्व इति विप्रर्षि रूरुं भित्त्वा व्यजायत–170–8). The *Harivaṃśa* speaks of one Urva of the Bhṛgu race who stretched forth his thigh into the fire. After rubbing it with a blade of Kuśa-grass there arose the fire *Aurva* (उर्वस्योरू विनिर्भिद्य और्वो नामान्तकोऽनलः–50). This Aurva was given shelter in the mouth of a mare. And Brahmā directed it to reside in the ocean. Besides *Matsya* referring to birth of Urvaśī from the thigh of Viṣṇu and *Skanda* (V. Avantikhaṇḍa (-1)9. 1–16) which speaks of the birth of Urvaśī from the thigh of Nara, all the Purāṇa texts like *Vāmana* (6. 1-3, 7. 1-20) *Devī Bhāgavata* (IV. 5–6) *Skanda* (V. Avantikhaṇḍa (-3) 192.5-193.66) are unanimous on the point that it is the sage Nārāyaṇa who produces from his thigh a beautiful damsel known as Urvaśī. This motif of the birth from the thigh is put differently in the *Viṣṇu–dharmottara Purāṇa* Part I. Ch. 129. With the sap of a mango tree Nārāyaṇa draws a picture of a woman on his thighs. Then, with the help of that drawing he gives birth to Urvaśī.

19. The *Padma* version differs from the *Matsya* only on this point. In all three versions in Padma (I.22) both Agastya and Vasiṣṭha are born from the semen of Mitra and Varuṇa.

20. जलकुम्भे ततो वीर्यं मित्रेण वरुणेन च,
प्रक्षिप्तमथ संजातौ द्वावेव मुनिसत्तमौ।
वसिष्ठोऽप्यभवत्तस्मिन् जलकुम्भे च पूर्ववत्।।
× × × × × × × ×
अगस्त्य इति शान्तात्मा बभूव मुनिसत्तमः।।
Matsya Purāṇa–Ch. 61.31.36

21. "It is noteworthy that no reason is given why Agastya was so born (born of Mitra Varuṇa), such as is given for Vasiṣṭha". *Indian Historical Tradition* P. 238. In face of this version of Matsya Ch.61 giving a logical account of the events leading to Agastya's birth from Mitra Varuṇa, I think the learned scholar's view is mistaken.

22. ततः कामयमानेन मित्रेणाहूय सोर्वशी।
उक्ता मां रमयस्वेति वाढमित्यब्रवीत्तु सा।।
गच्छन्ती चाम्बरं तद्वत् स्तोकमिन्दीवरेक्षणा।
वरुणेन धृता पश्चात् वरुणं नाभ्यनन्दत।। *Matsya* Ch. 61. 27–28

23. Also called *Nṛsiṃha* (or Narasiṃha) Purāṇa, it is one of the oldest and most important of the extant Vaiṣṇava Upa-Purāṇas. In the opinion of Hazra it must have been written not later than 850 A.D. (*Studies in Upa-Purāṇas,* Vol. I, P. 287). Kane puts it around 9 th century A.D.

24. According to Hazra, The *Narasiṃha Purāṇa* Ch. 6 dealing with the birth of Agastya and Vasiṣṭha is most probably comparatively late addition (*Studies in Upa-Purāṇas,* Vol. I, P. 252).

25. A verbatim repetition of *Bṛhaddevatā 152* which has been ignored by us on the authority of Macdonell. This reading is based on the manuscripts of 'B' group which contain later additions and naturally unreliable.

26. For a detailed discussion of Puṃsavana, *Hindu Saṃskāras* V.2; *India of Vedic Kalpasūtras,* p. 257-260.

27 इदं पुंसीयमाख्यानं वारुणं पापनाशनम्।
पुत्रकामास्तु ये केचिच्छृण्वन्तीदं शुचिव्रताः
अचिरादेव पुत्रांस्ते लभन्ते नात्र संशयः।।42।।

28. In *Ṛgveda* Varuṇa is the god of morality and righteousness. He is the up-holder of the cosmic order of the universe (*Ṛtasya patiḥ*). In the Vedic literature his relation with the rivers and the oceans is not

wanting and he is spoken of as sending rain and refreshment from the sky (RV.7.64.2; 8.25.6). In the MBH. (śalya parvan, Ch. 46.5-11) Varuṇa's position becomes conspicuous; he is conorated as the king of the waters. In *Rāmāyaṇa* (Uttarakāṇḍa ch. 3.9-18) along with Indra, Yama and Vaiśravaṇa he is appointed by Brahmā as the guardian of the quarters.

29. विवेश स तयोर्देहे मित्रावरुणयोः किल।
जीवांशेन वसिष्ठोऽथ त्यक्त्वा देहमनुत्तमम्।। VI. 14.59

30. मित्रावरुणकौ देवौ पुत्रवन्तौ महाद्युती। सिद्धिर्भविष्यति यथा युवयौर्वैष्णवी पुनः।39। स्वाधिकारेण स्थीयेतामधुना लोकसाक्षिकौ।

31. Vide Hariyappa, *Ṛgvedic Legends Through the Ages,* p. 288.

32. सूतो वा सूत पुत्रो वा यो वा को वा भवाम्यहम्।
दैवायत्तं कुले जन्म मदायत्तं हि पौरुषम्।।

33. तत्र जात्यान्तरजन्तुषु अनेकजातिसंभवा महर्षयो बहवः सन्ति। ऋष्यशृङ्गो मृग्याः, कौशिकः कुशात्, जाम्बूको जम्बुकात् वाल्मीको वल्मीकात्, व्यासः कैवर्तककन्यायाम्, शशपृष्ठात् गौतमः, वसिष्ठः उर्वश्याम्, अगस्त्यः कलशे जात इति श्रुतत्वात्। एतेषां जात्या विनाप्यग्रे ज्ञानप्रतिपादिता ऋषयो बहवः सन्ति।

Bibliography

1. *Ṛgvẽda Maṇḍala*–VII H.D. Velankar, Bharatiya Vidya Bhavan, Bombay, 1963.
2. *Atharvaveda Saṃhitā* (Text)–Ajmer, Vikram, Saṃvat, 2001.
3. *Atharvaveda-Saṃhitā*–Translated by W.D. Whitney, Harvard University, 1905.
4. *The Nighaṇṭu and Nirukta*–L. Sarup (Text & Trans.) Motilal Banarasidass, 1967.
5. *Bṛhaddevatā attributed to Śaunaka*–Part I (Introduction & Text); Part II (Trans. & Notes) A.A. Macdonell Motilal Banarasidass 1965.
6. *Ṛgveda-Sarvānukramaṇī of Kātyāyana and Anuvākānukramaṇī of Śaunaka*–Edited by U.C. Sharma, Viveka Publications, Aligarh, 1977.
7. *Mahābhārata* Vol. I, Vol. II, Vol. III, Vol. IV–Critically edited BORI, Poona, 1974.
8. *The Purāṇa Pañcalakṣaṇam* Text-W. Kirfel, edited by Suryakanta Sastri, Chowkhamba Sanskrit series Office, Varanasi, 1979.
9. Vāyu Purāṇa–Venkatesvara Press, Saṃvat, 1990.
10. *Brahmāṇḍa Purāṇa*–Venkatesvara Press, Saṃvat, 1992.

11. *Viṣṇu Purāṇa*–Gita Press, Gorakhapur, Saṃvat, 2033.
12. *Bhāgavata Purāṇa*–Gita Press, Gorakhpur, Saṃvat, 2037.
13. *Devī Bhāgavata Purāṇa*–Mansukhray Mor, Calcutta, 1961.
14. *Matsya Purāṇa*–Nandalal Mor, Calcutta, 1954.
15. *Viṣṇudharmottara Purāṇa*–Part I, Venkatesvara Press, Saṃvat, 1969.
16. *Padma Purāṇa*–Part I, Mansukhray Mor, Calcutta, 1957.
17. *Harivaṃśa*–Critical edition BORI, Poona, 1976.
18. *The Vāmana Purāṇa*–Edited by A.S. Gupta, All India Kashiraj Trust, 1968.
19. *Skanda Purāṇa*–Part V, Venkatesvara Press, Saṃvat, 1966.
20. *Indian Historical Tradition*–F.E. Pargiter, Oxford University Press, London, 1922.
21. *Narasiṃha Purāṇa*–Gopal Narayan & Co., Bombay, 1911.
22. *Studies in the Upa-Purāṇas*–Vol. I, R.C. Hazra, Sanskrit College, Calcutta, 1958.
23. *History of Dharmaśātra*–Vol. V, Part II, P. V. Kane, BORI, Poona.
24. *Hindū Saṃskāras*–R.B. Pandey, Motilal Banarsidass, 1976.
25. *India of Vedic Kalpasūtras*–Ram Gopal, National Publishing House, Delhi, 1959.
26. *Uttarakāṇḍa-Vālmīki-Rāmāyaṇa*–Edited by U.P. Shah, Oriental Institute, Baroda, 1975.
27. *Ṛgvedic Legends Through the Ages*–H.L. Hariyappa, Deccan College Post-Graduate & Research Institute, Poona, 1953.
28. *Upaniṣad Saṃgraha*–Edited by J.L. Sastri, Motilal Banarsidass, 1980.
29. *Veṇī Saṃhāra*–Edited by S. Viswanathan, Sri Balamanorama Press, Mylapore, Madras, 1961.